The Awakening

JENNIFER JAYDE

A Guide to Spiritually Awaken Your Highest Self,
Intuitive Connection, and Deepest Purpose.

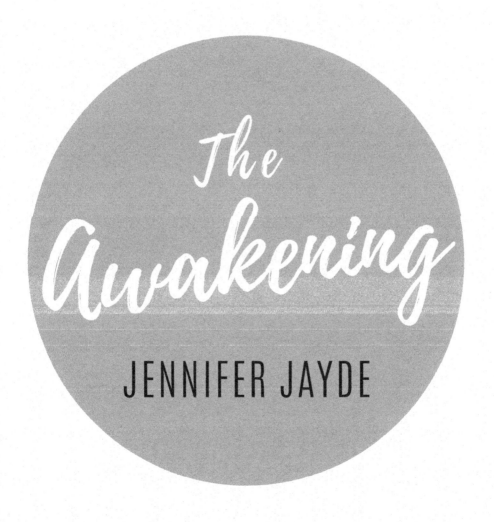

The
Awakening

JENNIFER JAYDE

DEDICATION

My first solo book is dedicated to my soul's greatest teachers in this life. Tricia Grey, for taking on the role as my Mother in
this life, and all the challenges that come along with being the
exact kind of woman I needed you to be, so that I could learn
how to become the kind of woman I wanted to be. Thank you.
I love you. Jack Hill Sr., for being my Dad, for teaching me so
much in so many more ways than you know. You never feel like
you've given me enough - and yet you've given me far more
than anything money could ever buy. You've given me love,
you've given me life, you've given me the world. Thank you. I
love you. Graham Spencer, my husband of 10 years, my best
friend, my person that makes me laugh every single day. You
balance me out, support me unconditionally, and have the kind
of inner and outer strength I admire. I've learned so much simply by being your wife, by being in your presence, and through
experiencing your love. The whole reason I've felt so free to fly,
is knowing that I always have a safe place to land. Thank you.
I love you. To my incredible bonus parents - Grace Hill, Laurie
Grey and Ron Guild - thank you for loving me like I was your
own, for being so generous with your affection, guidance and
love for me. Thank you for being apart of my life, I love you.
To Sarah Vanden Elsen, this book wouldn't even exist without
your swift loving kicks in the rear that I so need when my own
fears and ego are trying to get in my way. Thank you for being
my best friend/sister forever. You have been my guardian angel
almost my whole life. Thank you. I love you. ~ BF/SF~

Allison Taylor, Sarah Grey, Samantha McCarthy, John Hill and Joe Hill - thank you for allowing me the gift of being your big sister all these years. I've learned so much just from watching you grow into the amazing human beings you are today. My heart is so full just from being apart of your life. I am in awe of you. Thank you. I love you.

And to my soul-mentor - the late Wayne Dyer. Thank you for teaching me what it means to live an inspired life when I needed it most. Thank you for living and loving the way you did, and continue to do. For a man that was magical with his words, I am at a loss to describe. Thank you will never be enough. I meant what I promised you, and I hope this book brings a smile to your soul. Thank you. I love you.

~ In loving memory of those I love that have gone home before me - who remind me every day how precious each moment is, and how every day I wake up alive is a gift. That it is an honour and a privilege to see another birthday, not a curse. That I would rather try and fail at something I love, than to never know what could've been. Nana on the beach, Grandma Christina, Grandma Ruby, Grandpa Jack, Grandma Bev, Gramps, Dan Nelson, Garrett Paquette, Don Mikado, Karen Mikado. Thank you, I love you ~

CONTENTS

PART 4 - AWAKENING YOUR PURPOSE

PART 5 - ALIGNING YOUR SOUL FOR ULTIMATE SUCCESS

Foreword

I have to say that being asked to write this foreword took me back to being 7 years old and watching my dad (Dr. Wayne Dyer) write his first book, Your Erroneous Zones. I know he struggled with the decision to leave a tenured position and all of the security that a position like that created for our family. I remember how excited he was about the completion of each phase of his book and all of the chances he took in his life to make his vision a reality. I was a little girl, but I got to watch from the passenger seat while my dad turned his beliefs in to something tangible and turned one book in to the best selling book of the 1970's. Ultimately he turned all of his books and talks in to a lifetime of learning and teaching. The beginning of that journey was pretty grass roots. We drove across the United States during the summer of 1976 and I watched my dad get himself booked on every little radio & TV show across the country. When we finally arrived in California, he had figured out how to get himself on to the Tonight Show with Johnny Carson. Through a series of crazy coincidences and some sheer determination, he turned that appearance in to three appearances in one month. He did tell a horrible "training bra" story about me on the Tonight Show – keep in mind, I was in 5th grade and I was not happy about that story being told on national TV - he clearly didn't understand how embarrassing that was to an 11 year-old. I ultimately did forgive him and I've grown to be so grateful for those experiences and all of the lessons of determination and persistence that I learned along way.

Jennifer is at the beginning of her own teaching journey and in many ways her path has mirrored my fathers. She started down a path that she thought everyone should travel if they wanted to achieve success and happiness. She sought a high-pressure corporate career and all of the trappings that came with that choice, only to discover that real happiness couldn't be bought or harnessed unless she honored her own internal calling. I went down that path too and had to find my way back to my true creative calling - I loved the journey, all of the lessons and all of the friends I made along way – they have given beauty and meaning to my life. The biggest lesson I've learned along the way, is it is NEVER too late to make a huge shift, or as my dad was famous for saying to so many – "Don't die with your music still inside of you!" Jennifer has written a guide to discovering your own intuition and harnessing it to guide you along your own path. Intuition is something that I not only believe everyone can tune in to for themselves, but something that I actually KNOW you must tune in to in order to hear your own truth and to ultimately sing your own song.

I met Jennifer in Toronto in 2016. It was through an act of courage and following her own intuition that she decided to be brave and take a chance. She came over to me at a conference and I was deep in conversation with someone else. Jennifer walked away and later told me that she was intimidated. Now I am not famous and no one should ever be intimidated to strike up a conversation with me, but my father was a hero to her and she was projecting that on me. She went back in to the auditorium and she gathered up her own strength, and she listened to the small voice in her head, she came back out and tried again. This time she succeed-ed. I thought she was delightful and we ended up having a fabulous conversation about Moby Dick – one of my father's favorite books. Jennifer then reached out to me via email and she asked if I would consider writing the foreword to a book that she was working on, I said I would consider it, but only if I could read it first. I mention this story only because some-times the timing doesn't feel right in life or the circumstances don't feel safe, but that is exactly the time that you need to tune in to your inner voice the most. Get quiet, find your courage and bravely ask the world for what you want. The universe has a way of showing up just exactly as you ask it to.

Take a chance, learn from a teacher and tune in to your still quiet voice. Jennifer's wisdom and experiences can help to guide your way.

This is the quote that Jenner and I discussed in Toronto – it was one that my father used as fuel and it's ultimately what brought the two of us together – I hope it brings you joy.

"…For as this appalling ocean surrounds the verdant land, so in the soul of man there lies one insular Tahiti, full of peace and joy, but encompassed by all the horrors of the half-known life."   Herman Melville

Congratulations Jennifer on this huge accomplishment – hope your words help to change the world.

Peace and Joy,

Tracy Dyer

Preface

It took me investing over $100k in coaching, conferences, workshops, seminars, books, classes, and masterminds before I discovered the answers I really needed, I could have had for free.

I'd always been a go-getter. Always wanting to know more, do more, and be more. When I was still barely able to spell, I started my first business - Kool-aid stands.

Then I assisted my neighborhood friend with her paper route, because I was too young to legally have my own.

When I was old enough, I got two.

I expected myself to color within the lines by kindergarten, so much so that my teacher called my mom in to talk to her about how hard I was on myself when I didn't.

I expected myself to get straight A's in high school, while playing on three soccer teams and working four shifts a week at the local movie theatre.

And when I had the inner nudge to pursue photography after graduation, I stifled it because I didn't believe it would bring me the financial success and freedom that I desired in life.

Instead, I went into finance as a mortgage broker at age twenty- one, checking off all the boxes I thought would bring me happiness. A nice car, a nice house, a nice husband, and a successful career.

And after spending nearly all of my twenties grinding it out to make this happen, feeling like a small fish trying to swim upstream with all the big boys, I realized that no matter how much "success" I achieved, or how many of these boxes I checked off, I still wasn't happy.

And that is when I knew I had it all wrong.

I was running after something, chasing it as fast as I could, and yet finally awakening to the fact I had been sprinting down the wrong path all along.

If you resonate in any way with feeling like the life you've created is falling short of fulfilling you in a deep, meaningful way, this book is for you.

If you resonate in any way with searching for answers end-lessly in books, workshops, conferences, coaches, and the like, and still feel like something is missing, this book is for you.

And if you are ready to feel fully aligned with your soul, guided along your highest path, and connected with the infinite, limitless life force within you, this book is *most definitely* for you.

The spiritual path is
simply the journey of
living our lives. Everyone is on a
spiritual path;
most people just
don't know it.
~ Marianne Williamson

Introduction

The word "spirituality" gets tossed around so frequently these days, it's hard to know what it really means, and better yet, how we can truly practice it for our highest benefit.

To me, spirituality is the practice of getting to know one's true self, deep down on a Soul level, so we may live in alignment with our Highest Potential, our purpose. By doing so, we become a beacon of light, hope, and love for those around us, and for the world.

I believe the higher your joy, the brighter your light.

This book is designed to help you do just that - uncover your most powerful essence, connect with the infinite Source within you, and align with the clearest, most limitless version of you.

And in doing so, you will inspire others to do the same.

The Awakening is for anyone seeking to know the truth of who they really are, the Source from which they came, and how they can step more fully into all that they are capable of becoming in this life.

The Awakening

Whether you are newly exploring what spirituality means to you, or are a seasoned spiritual seeker, this book will take you to your personal next level of Awakening.

You may feel called to read these chapters in order from beginning to end, or you may choose to read whichever one is calling your soul today. Use your intuition to guide you - it always knows the way.

As for me, when I was disconnected from my spirituality, I was at the lowest point in my life. I was using my head to lead the way, and I found myself charging through life like a bull - grinding, hustling, and constantly rushing to get to the next finish line without any regard to the beauty, love, and blessings around me.

I was impatient, mean, and hard on myself - living under constant self-inflicted pressure, and always disappointed after missing the unrealistic deadlines and expectations I'd placed on my own shoulders.

By age twenty-four, I had a successful career in finance, two real estate properties, a big wedding at a castle, my fur baby, a convertible, shopping sprees, and some great travel experiences under my belt. All the things that I was racing toward since I was five years old, which was when I started my first Kool-Aid stand business after realizing my mom and I were poor.

Yet even after racing through the years ticking everything I could think of off my happiness to-do list, I was miserable.

How could this be?

My quest to discover the answer to this question sparked the beginning of my conscious spiritual journey, and over the course of the next few years, my life was dramatically altered for the better.

It all began with a realization that no matter how much my income level increased in my corporate finance job, my level of fulfillment and joy continued to decrease.

This realization took me through two career changes and helped me start my own businesses. I learned to lead with my soul instead of my mind and created a life far beyond what I'd ever imagined was possible for me when I was still stuck within those four windowless finance walls - all within just a few years.

When I (hesitantly) left hustling and grinding behind in favor of staying aligned with my spiritual beliefs and practice, I was able to see my actual purpose in life. For the very first time, I was able to trust my intuitive guidance and create from my soul. This led to me having more abundance, freedom, and fulfilment than I've ever known before.

This came in the form of physical things, like moving to my dream beach city after years of thinking it wasn't possible for me. Like starting a business based on something I loved so much I'd do it for free! Like facing fears and the liberating feeling that soon rushed in afterwards. Like reaching income levels higher than anyone in my family history within twelve months. Like purchasing my dream vision board luxury vehicle, without planning or forcing. Like being requested for TV interviews in both Canada and the New York without any publicists or forced efforts. Like a book offer that turned into an international best seller and award winner. Like being asked to speak all around North America, and paid to attend and speak at tropical retreats. This all happened within twenty-four months and without forced effort, hustling, or grinding.

But most importantly, it came in the form of feeling more alive, on-purpose, and fulfilled than I ever had before. Like I finally knew why I was born, and felt the joy of actually aligning with it!

These things (and many more) happened as a result of my spiritual Awakening, growth, and practices.

And this is what I want for you, dear soul, who is reading this.

For you to uncover the power that is within you, that may have been buried for far too long now under the myths and illusions of fear, society, and ego.

For you to connect with your Highest Self again and again and again - for guidance, for reassurance, for clarity, for trust.

For you to live your life the way your soul intended you to.

For you to Awaken . . .

In this book, you will learn everything that has helped me create and live a life beyond my wildest dreams within the last two years:

- how to connect and dialogue with your most trusted soul advisors through the use of your Intuition
- how to distinguish between a fear-based "no" and an intuitive, soul-aligned "no"
- the shortcut to manifesting (it's not as time-consuming as you think!)

- how to understand, identify, and disempower ego, and empower your Highest level of being instead
- how to uncover your Purpose in this life
- how to clear, cleanse, protect, and boost your personal energy
- how to align with your Soul to reach your desires with more ease and less resistance
- how to truly awaken your wealth consciousness and receive more money and abundance than you ever have before
- how to identify the deeper hidden ways you've been holding yourself back, so you can finally set yourself free to be, do, and have all that is waiting for you!

If you're ready to remember and rediscover just how powerful you truly are, if you're ready to learn some new techniques, tips, practices, and insights into how you can evolve even further, and if you're ready to step into the mostly highly aligned, awakened, limitless version of you - you're in the right place.

Welcome to the Awakening, dear friend!

She who looks outside dreams. She
who looks inside, awakens . . .
~ Carl Jung

1

Awakening Your Intuition

CHAPTER 1

Yes, You Are Intuitive

"The more you trust your intuition, the more empowered
you become, the stronger you become, and
the happier you become."
~ Gisele Bündchen

As far back as I can remember, I was always mesmerized by psychics and mediums. My mom and I shared this fascination and would often go for readings whenever the opportunity arose as a fun thing to do together. Then we'd happily discuss afterwards if we felt they were the "real deal" or not.

I read books about them, their lives, and how they came to discover their extraordinary gifts. I watched them on TV - *John Edwards*, *Long Island Medium*, etc. And I often thought to myself how cool it would be to have an inside perspective on life and the best choices to make for myself at any given moment.

Meanwhile, I was busy chasing the almighty dollar. Unknowingly, yet blatantly, ignoring an inner niggling to pursue photography in exchange for the belief that once I was earning lots of money in finance, I would be free. Free of worry, free of struggle, and happy as could be.

As a child, I'd watched my single mom pace around our little run-down basement suite on the phone, trying to hide her panic over how rent would be paid each month. She began having her first bouts of anxiety and panic attacks around this time. She did a good job of trying to hide it, but there weren't many places to hide in our little home.

That's when the Kool-aid stands started, and when my sole focus became success.

It turns out I wasn't running toward something. I was running away from it. The fear of scarcity and lack - and as fast as I possibly could.

But the further I ran down this path, the further away I actually felt from happiness - and it baffled me.

By now, I'd checked off all the boxes I thought would bring me the happiness, the success, the *relief* I'd always wanted - and yet it couldn't have felt further from the truth.

What had I done? And what was I supposed to do now? Would I ever be happy? I wish I was psychic.

Okay, I thought - *maybe my happiness won't come from my job, but I can create some on my evenings and weekends.*

As soon as I went to purchase my first DSLR camera since

my old high school days of point-and-shoots, I felt this inner glow of excitement inside of me. Like something in me was saying, "Yes!"

This feeling began to grow each time I learned something new with my camera, took a photo I loved, or did a shoot for friends. And it reached an exhilarating high after photographing my first-ever wedding. *People get paid to do something this fun?!*

Around this time, Oprah was airing her final episode of *The Oprah Winfrey Show*, and I'll never forget the words she shared as she closed out twenty-five years of her own personal passion:

"Even before I had a name for it, I could feel the voice bigger than myself, speaking to me. And all of us have that same voice. Be still and know it. You can acknowledge it or not. You can worship it or not. You can praise it, you can ignore it, or you can know it. Know it. It's always there, speaking to you, and waiting for you to hear it. In every move, in every decision, I wait, and I listen. I am still. I wait and listen for the guidance that's greater than my meager mind. The only time I've ever made mistakes is when I didn't listen. So what I know is . . . life is always speaking to you. First in whispers. It's subtle, those whispers. And if you don't pay attention to the whispers, it gets louder and louder. It's like getting a thump upside the head. If you don't pay attention to that, it's like getting a brick upside the head. You don't listen to that, eventually the whole brick wall comes tumbling down. And so I ask you, what are the whispers in your life right now? What's whispering to you, and will you hear it. Your life is whispering to you, what is it saying?"

My life had been whispering to me for almost a decade

now to pursue photography. But I didn't listen. I put my nose to the grindstone, but even as my success grew, I became increasingly unhappy. I became lethargic, low-energy, and increasingly uninterested in life, wondering if this was all there was.

Until I picked up a camera again. It felt like the Universe was leaving me a trail of bigger and bigger joy-crumbs, the more I followed the things that excited me.

When I heard Oprah share these words, I'd also had a recent wake-up call from the sudden loss of a loved one. I was at a tipping point where I just couldn't bear to keep walking down the finance path any longer.

I realized that I would have regret on my deathbed if I didn't find out what could have been with photography, and that we never actually know when our time is up.

So over the course of a year, I learned everything I possibly could, both about the business side of photography and the creative art of being a photographer, and I transitioned into a whole new life.

Often in life, we forego what we already know to be true in our hearts, for safety. Safety from what others might think, safety from failing, safety from lack and scarcity, safety from fear. We use excuses disguised as reasons for why we stay still, safe, and stuck.

For me, this began to feel like dying a slow, painful death. The fire in my soul was dimming to barely burning embers with each and every passing day. Instead of getting closer to happiness and fulfilment, like I once thought I would be, I was actually getting further and further away.

Only when I began to grow curious about what my inner whispering was saying to me, did things change.

In a short span of time (and pushing beyond my greatest inner fears), I would grow a successful destination wedding photography business, garner awards for my work, and be hired to travel to my dream locations in Hawaii, Australia, and the Caribbean.

After just three years, I would feel called to move into coaching other women to discover, create, and live their own dream lives and businesses, and that journey would generate six figures in sales in its first six months of operation and a quarter million in the first year. Within eighteen months, I would go on to be interviewed dozens of times online and twice on TV in both Canada and the US, become an internationally best-selling author, and feel more aligned with my self, my purpose, and my happiness than ever before.

With 20/20 hindsight, I know that my greatest growth and happiness comes from following my inner whispering, my inner guide, my intuition - daily.

And I know the devastating mistakes I've made along the way happened when I wasn't listening.

I realized we don't have to be psychic in order to get "inside information" about the quickest path to our ultimate joy.

The truth is, we are all limitless, infinite beings temporarily occupying a human vessel and visiting this soul playground until it's time to go back to our infinite home.

We are not separate from where we come from; our soul

is still connected to this infinite place and is *receiving guidance from it 24/7.*

It's our human self who must decide whether or not we want to listen, and if we do listen, whether or not we dare trust it and take action without seeing the whole picture in advance.

With every single choice we find ourselves at a crossroads with, we're given the free will to choose - *Will I move forward in faith, or will I step backward in fear?*

If you're reading this book, I know the Universe guided you to it. And I know it's for a reason.

You are being called to listen, to take inspired action, and to move forward in faith.

You can feel it in your heart, can't you?

That feeling that something is missing, something hasn't quite clicked into place yet.

That you're meant for so much more.

Maybe you relate to following the wrong voice in the past - the one that says you don't have time to pursue your dreams, or that you'll never make enough money with it, or that you don't have anything meaningful to offer the world. That you're not educated enough, smart enough, talented enough, or pretty enough to be successful in a fulfilling, joyful, powerful way.

My friend, if you resonate with any of this, you're in the right place.

We're about to uncover your connection to your infinite inner guide, your Intuition. Together, we'll deepen it, strengthen it, and get you consciously attached to the infinite source within you, so you can create the limitless, purposeful, fulfilling, and most soul-aligned life you were truly born to live.

Our best guide, is inside.
~ Jennifer Jayde

CHAPTER 2

Connecting To Your Intuition

"Intuition is seeing with the soul."
~ Dean Koontz

My desire to be able to receive "inside information" like the famous psychics and mediums I loved learning about actually derailed me from realizing I did have access to this information all along.

I thought that I had to see visions and symbols in my mind, or hear spirits talking to me, or be able to use tarot cards or something along those lines. I had "Hollywood"-sized my expectations and interpretations of what intuition was, making it feel like it was out of reach for an ordinary girl like me. That it was an extraordinary gift reserved just for a select few.

In fact, when I realized how my own intuition was working within me, I was underwhelmed and yet at the same time, also very excited.

The Awakening

In the beginning, before I would even call it intuition, I realized I had two very different voices that would surface inside my head, especially when I was facing any big life decisions.

One voice would feel excited, intrigued, and inspired to move forward with whatever new path was presenting itself. Then the other voice would come storming in with a sh*t storm of reasons why there was no way I should even consider this right now.

For most of my life, I'd listened to the latter.

The one that told me to get a good job, buy a nice house, get a nice husband, get a cute fur baby, and all would be well. To play it safe, to take the career that would afford me the best lifestyle. The one that told me I'd be a starving artist if I even *considered* photography as a career. The one that said I'd never be as good, successful, or happy as other people who were highly educated, wealthy, and fit.

After nearly a decade, I realized that I had let this voice lead me to a place I wasn't happy with whatsoever (even when I had done exactly what it instructed me to do). I began questioning this voice and finally started shifting from finance to photography.

And it was during this shift that I started paying closer attention to the other voice.

The one that said - *Yes, you can. Yes, you will. Give it a try! Why not?*

This voice was much more subtle, kinder, and gentler. It wasn't as easy to hone in on at first because the other voice was so wildly loud and boisterous inside my mind. The other voice played on my fears and was obnoxiously persistent with getting me to listen to it.

But the more I listened to the softer, gentler, kinder voice, the more I began trusting it.

The more I began to see that everywhere it led me felt amazing, even if I had to walk forward in spite of the fear-voice trying to stop me.

And as I developed more trust in this softer voice, I was that much more aware of her presence and recognized it more clearly the next time I heard it. And again and again.

The less energy I gave to my mean voice, *the less power* it had over me.

And I realized if I stopped for a moment and dropped my thoughts from my head to my heart, I could receive guidance in any given moment - about *anything*.

I could tune in about which route to take home; I could tune in about what outfit to wear each morning; I could tune in for what words to use for a hurting friend or what gifts to buy my loved ones at Christmas.

More often than not, when I tuned in to this soft inner guidance, I would end up receiving subtle validation later on about why that guidance was given to me (though I've also learned to trust it even when the proof isn't there).

In the case of which route to drive home, often I would later hear about bad traffic or an accident on the route I normally take.

In the case of which outfit to wear, often the outfit I originally planned to wear was actually better suited for the next day or a day later when a friend invited me out to dinner. Or I would spill something on myself later that day, and I would've been wearing my favorite white jeans had I not listened.

In the case of what words to say to a friend, those words were often followed with, "Well it's funny you say that, because . . ."

And in the case of buying gifts for loved ones, they would wonder how I knew what they wanted or whether their spouse had secretly told me what to buy for them.

It felt fun and good, and it made everything that much more meaningful.

When I shifted into photography, I would tune into this inner voice / inner feeling about what clients would be pleasant to work with and which ones to avoid.

I would tune into it about pricing and what to include in my packages.

It would even guide me during photo shoots, with the right words to use and questions to ask to make a couple feel more comfortable - and even how to pose them and capture the images in the most authentic and beautiful way possible.

For the first time in my life, I felt like I knew what it meant to be "in flow" with the Universe.

Though that wouldn't always be the case.

I'm not perfect when it comes to staying in flow 24/7 or

always being able to tune in accurately 100% of the time.

Sometimes I get distracted or I overthink things so much, I can no longer tell which voice is my head and which voice is my heart.

And there was a time when I would put the opinions of experts ahead of my own inner guidance. That cost me a lot.

Remember when I said I've invested over $100k in search of answers I could have had for free? Not only did I spend way more money than I even had to my name (going into debt and applying for more credit so I could max that out, too - yikes!), but I spent so much of something I value even more than money - my time.

Yet again, I'd derailed myself by looking for, and listening to, everyone else outside of myself to give me the answers that would satisfy my soul.

And I couldn't find those answers, no matter how much I paid. So I would spend more, and more, and more.

It was almost like a gambler at a casino - I felt like I needed to go all in to see the return I wanted.

But in reality, I need to go all INSIDE.

Finally, when the debt had piled up to the roof and I was emotionally, spiritually, and physically spent, I had two choices - keep digging myself into a deeper hole, or take a step back and really look at the bigger picture of what was happening here.

I stopped working with my high-end business coach. I took

a break from conferences, workshops, even self-help books.

I needed to quiet the voices of others and tune back into the voice of my soul.

This is when everything began to change.

Where I once felt like the gas was leaking out of my tank, my inspiration was fading, and my mood and energy were deflating - I now felt something spark within me once again.

I heard that soft, loving voice again.

It reminded me of who I am, what I stand for, what I'm capable of, and what excites me.

It showed me that I had taken a bit of a detour where my finances and my purpose were concerned, but lovingly reminded me it was all part of a greater lesson that was in service to me.

And when I connected to what would excite me now, a flood of inspired ideas came rushing through me.

I felt alive again. Clear and bright again. On fire again. On purpose again.

And now, my friend, it's your turn.

There may be some questions in your life you've been seeking the answers to for quite some time.

Maybe you're wondering what your purpose is.

Maybe you're wondering how you can feel more fulfilled,

and whether your life has a true and deep meaning behind it.

Maybe you're anxious to know how you can finally feel and become more successful in life.

And maybe the countless books, workshops, conferences, masterminds, coaches, mentors, etc. haven't been able to provide you with that piece of clarity you've been yearning for.

They've helped, yes, but maybe there's still a piece of the puzzle that hasn't quite fallen into place yet.

You can't put your finger on what it is, but you know it's there.

If this is you, may you find relief in knowing you no longer have to walk down this path. The answers you are seeking cannot be found in any of these places or from any other person - no matter how highly educated, trained, or esteemed they are.

What we're going to uncover next will guide you through the process of finding your deepest soul truths on your own. Not just today, but every day, for the rest of your life.

Because you are truly the only one who can find them.

Are you ready?

You cannot go from where
you are to where you want to
be by asking anyone outside of you
what is the proper path.
Religion cannot give it to you.
Politics cannot give it to you.
Your mother cannot give it to you.
Your teacher cannot give it to you.
No one can give you accurate guid-
ance, but no one needs to
because you have built in guidance.
~ Abraham Hicks

CHAPTER 3

Discovering Your Unique Intuitive Language

"The intuitive mind is a sacred gift and the rational mind is a faithful servant. We have created a society that honors the servant and has forgotten the gift."
~ Albert Einstein

Remember how I said I was actually a little underwhelmed (though still very excited) to discover how my own intuition worked?

Picture this . . .

I was having a really odd week when I felt like the Universe was trying to tell me something, and I just couldn't get it. I was having really odd dreams, I was seeing the same "signs" everywhere, and I just had that overall feeling like when someone is trying to speak to you in a foreign language and you just can't quite grasp what they're trying to say.

I felt this growing inner frustration, and even wondered if I was going crazy.

I knew I had to relax, so I went to my two staples - a good book and the beach. I spent all Sunday afternoon with both.

I came home feeling a tad better, but not completely relieved . . . and I started watching the latest episode of a new show called, *Tyler Henry, Hollywood Medium*.

I watched him as he was able to scribble down signs and symbols coming into his mind's eye and translate them into clear messages from beyond for his clients.

I was in awe. I'd seen people do this before, but this time was different. It really made me curious about whether that could ever be possible for me, even in some small way.

Could I ever do that? I randomly thought to myself.

And then I heard this inner whisper say, *Would you like to know how you receive messages?*

And my next inner thought was - *YES!*

You hear them Jen, you HEAR them! Just like you are, right now.

WHAT!!! Mind blown!

Then I did what any millennial girl would do - I went straight to Google.

And that's when I realized that being intuitive isn't reserved for the famous psychics and mediums on TV. We are all connected to divine inner guidance - just in varying degrees of clarity and in our own unique way.

This made me feel both underwhelmed (*What? That's really it? I've been doing it all along?*) and excited to grow and expand this new-found ability.

I became obsessed with learning more about these extra-sensory languages and developing my own understanding even further.

From what we know at this stage of human awareness, there are six main "clairs" or clear channels of intuition. People are commonly more dominant in one or two. As you develop your intuition, you may even activate additional clairs as you go!

Once you can connect to your most dominant one or two intuitive language types, you can then move on to receiving your guidance more clearly and effectively, and strengthen your ability to be guided more easily and effortlessly along your highest path.

Here are the main four clairs I most commonly come across in people I meet or work with:

Clairaudience

Also means "clear hearing."

This is not to say you hear voices audibly outside of your head (although perhaps you have!). More than likely, these intuitive downloads, thoughts, epiphanies, and "ah-ha" moments actually sound like your own voice / thoughts inside your mind.

The difference is, you have no explanation for where these "out of the blue" insights came from.

They came from your inner guide!

Because this inner guidance often resembles our own thoughts, chances are you've been having inner dialogue and guidance like this your whole life without even realizing it. You may have even experienced ringing in your ears at times and may be easily annoyed / distracted by sounds and noises around you.

Clairvoyance

Means "clear seeing."

Just like with clairaudience, you likely do not see things visibly outside of you (although you may). Rather, these intuitive downloads, thoughts, epiphanies, and "ah-ha" moments typically come to you in images through your mind's eye, dreams, or flashes of thought, just like a visual memory of something you'd seen in the past.

You have no explanation for where these "out of the blue" visuals come from.

These too come from your inner guide!

These inner visions often resemble our own visualizations, and chances are you've been seeing inner visions like these your whole life without even realizing it. As a result, you may not have been understanding the symbols your intuitive self is trying to share with you.

Clairvoyance can actually be so subtle that it may feel like you're imagining or making it up in your head. You don't even have to close your eyes to have this type of inner "seeing."

For example, if I said, "Picture a red truck with a white roof," you'd be able to "see" that in your mind's eye without even closing your eyes.

You likely tend to be more of a visual person when it comes to giving or taking directions and ideas, and you appreciate visual beauty and surroundings more than most. You may have even seen flashes of light or orbs in your peripheral vision.

Claircognizance

Means "clear knowing."

Your intuitive downloads come to you most dominantly through light bulb flashes of "instant knowing" that seemingly come out of nowhere.

Only of course, they came from somewhere - your inner guide!

Because these sudden inner realizations often resemble our own thoughts, chances are you've been having inner guidance like this your whole life without even realizing it.

Claircognizance can actually be the most doubted intuitive connection (at first) because it takes practice to differentiate between a hint from your intuition and your own normal thoughts. Claircognizant information comes to you as a quick and sudden flash of light, bringing answers and instincts immediately, without any chance for developing a thought over time. And just as suddenly as this intuitive epiphany arrives (often when we are not even trying for it, such as while in the shower or exercising), it can vanish. This makes it a good idea to write these things down ASAP!

You have an unquiet mind and tend to think quite a lot. You have lots of sudden ideas that you can't wait to share, and you often even interrupt others - you can't help it! When you meet someone, you know whether or not they are trust-worthy without any explanation. And you often prefer learn-ing through books or written words.

Clairsentience

Means "clear feeling."

Your intuitive downloads come to you most dominantly through gut feelings or chills, or through sensing the emo-tions of others.

These feelings and sensations came from your inner guide!

Because these inner feelings often resemble our own feel-ings, chances are you've been having inner guidance like this your whole life without even realizing it!

The difference is, clairsentient information comes to you as an internal feeling or emotion that doesn't have any real justification for being your own.

You are highly in tune with your own emotions often describing things by feeling, for example, "This doesn't feel right," or "This feels like a yes for me."

And you are also very in tune with the emotions of others. This can be quite draining physically and emotionally, and can lead you to feel exhausted for no reason when protective measures haven't been taken in advance. It's also very important to clear your energy each day in order to get rid of excess emotions you "picked up" the day before or overnight.

While your intuitive insights feel like a totally natural part of you, not everyone receives their intuitive insights in the same way.

Now that you know what your strongest intuitive connection is, I highly recommend that you pay attention to it and develop it further. This will be your greatest guide, asset, and tool as you move forward in creating a fulfilling, meaningful, and exhilarating life!

In short, There is nothing else anywhere, There is not a set of rules,
There are not a stack of books,
There are not teachers,
There are not hidden documents,
There is nothing outside of you
that can come anywhere close to
the guidance that comes forth
from within you.

~ Abraham Hicks

Gift For You:

Head over to
http://www.jenniferjayde.com/theawakeningbook
and download your free Intuition Guide that will
walk you through the steps to developing your
own Intuitive language starting today!

CHAPTER 4

How To Strengthen Your Intuition

"Like a GPS, your intuition doesn't come and go or stop and start randomly; it's always on and working for you throughout your journey. And it will always redirect you back onto your highest path no matter which seemingly wrong turn you may take."
~ Jennifer Jayde

After learning that not only was I intuitive (that we all are), but also what my own specific intuitive language was, I wanted to know more! How could I get even clearer guidance? How could I get "better" at being clairaudient?

And after taking the long route, I discovered that in order to become better at your language, you need to learn to trust it more. Trust is how your intuition grows in strength and clarity.

It happens by paying attention to those subtle inner nudges, trusting them, taking inspired action on behalf of them even when you don't fully understand **why** and even when ego is trying to stop you or slow you down, and getting through to the other side - where you realize, yet again, your soul was right.

Again, and again, and again.

With the small things (where you will actually find a parking space, or which friend to message a friendly "hello") and with the big things (career moves, starting and growing your dream business, big life transitions and decisions).

Again, and again, and again.

By far, building *trust* and taking inspired action in alignment with this trust will be your biggest asset in growing your intuitive connection.

But there are definitely some things that will make this learning process even easier . . .

Meditation

Deepak Chopra says, *"Prayer is you speaking to God. Meditation is allowing the Spirit to speak to you, but it speaks in silence and it then manifests as intuition."*

Imagine someone you knew and loved was feeling overwhelmed, stressed, upset, and depleted over a situation going on in her life. And imagine you actually had a helpful piece of advice or perspective to share with her that you knew would help alleviate her frustration and inner pain.

But this friend never, ever, ever stopped talking. She would never let you speak. She would cut you off, interrupt you, distract herself with her phone or work, or talk about how hungry she was or how she needed a glass of wine.

There was never a space for you to come in and give her the insights, perspective, or helpful guidance that would truly help her move forward with ease and joy.

This is what it's like when we avoid silence and stillness.

Our intuition, our connection to infinite intelligence and love, is always there, always willing, and always attempting to give us soulful guidance. In any given moment of every day.

Yet often, we're too busy talking with friends, lost in our own mind's chitter chatter, or distracting ourselves with what we think will make us feel better - whether that be food, alcohol, caffeine, sugar, shopping, or TV - or cultivating sources of external validation such as social media, winning awards, making more money, hitting certain milestones in our career, being mommy, wife, or daughter of the year, and the list goes on.

We rapidly race to fill this "void" with things outside of ourselves, when really, all we need to do is listen. Our inner guide is speaking to us, and it is always coming from a place of love. It is nothing to fear or try to avoid.

Everyone can meditate. I know this because I was the most avid believer of the opposite being true. I figured my mind was just too busy and my life was just too busy and there was no way I could ever meditate. I truly believed it just wasn't for me.

In reality, I was avoiding.

There is always time for what we prioritize. Always. No excuses.

If all you can manage right now is a sixty second pause to focus on your breath - awesome. If you can find a five-minute guided meditation you enjoy on Youtube - great!

The truth is, though, I've learned that even the busiest people in the world often meditate for at least twenty minutes in silence every day - usually first thing in the morning.

You don't have to start out this way, but do use it as a compass and build momentum in this direction if you desire to tune in more clearly to your Intuition.

Who meditates, you ask?

A quick list of those who have acknowledged the benefits of meditation in their life (and this list doesn't even represent a sliver of those who practice around the globe):

- Oprah Winfrey
- Tony Robbins
- Katy Perry
- Gabby Bernstein
- Jerry Seinfeld
- Hugh Jackman
- Mick Jagger
- Paul McCartney
- Heather Graham
- Jennifer Aniston
- Russell Brand
- Gisele Bündchen
- Ellen DeGeneres
- Cameron Diaz

- Lena Dunham
- Tim Ferriss
- Tom Hanks
- Jennifer Lopez
- Amy Schumer
- Jenna Dewan-Tatum
- Kate Hudson
- Dr. Oz

After spending some time wandering in and out of practicing different kinds of meditations, I came across Transcendental Meditation, and something told me to pay attention. The Universe was repeatedly bringing Transcendental Meditation into my awareness, and I knew from experience that repetition from the Universe is never coincidental.

So I found the nearest Transcendental Meditation center and invested in learning this meditation technique.

It was absolutely the right fit for me. My intuition didn't steer me wrong (of course), and I've found even greater clarity during the twenty minutes when I ease into meditation every morning.

I find I am much calmer throughout the day. Things that used to get under my skin just don't seem as bothersome anymore. I no longer feel the need to be perfect or to win everyone's approval before making a decision of my own. I feel much more clearly guided, and I receive answers to deep, meaningful questions that seem to elude me when my mind is more distracted during the day.

I feel a lot more at ease and at peace with my journey. At the same time, meditation seems to help close the time gap between my reality and my desired intentions because I am no longer lost in the fog of guessing and wondering. Rather, I am more clearly guided each and every day.

If you're not in the habit of meditating daily but would love to welcome the benefits of this practice into your life, start with finding some free guided meditations online. Find a space where you can sit comfortably and quietly and focus on your breath. It's okay if your mind wants to fire up your thoughts, worries, to-do list, etc. When these things come up, just gently return your focus to your breathing. Again, and again, and again. Eventually your mind will grow to understand this is a time for silence and deep connection between your soul and Source, and it won't be so turbulent anymore.

I have also heard great things about a meditation app called Headspace.

And if you're feeling called to explore a learned type of meditation practice, make sure you go with your intuition in finding which one feels right for you.

Intuitive Journaling

Okay, so this can be *really* fun and eye-opening. Now that you know your intuitive language, journaling can be a lot more expansive and insightful than it used to be - I *love* doing this!

Best done right after a meditation, a few minutes of journaling can go a *long* way.

No matter what you have on your mind on a given day, this is an incredible time to get curious about what your intuition is trying to teach you, guide you to, or bring to your attention right now.

You could start by asking the question and then allowing your soul's loving responses to move through your hand, through your pen, and onto your page - without judgement (ego interference). No thinking, no stalling, just writing with flow - whatever your first instinct is, let it flow onto the paper. The less you filter, the more powerful and accurate your intuitive responses will be.

Ideally, frame your question in an empowering way that helps give you clarity on how to move forward, rather than just giving you reasons for why you feel this way currently and leaving it at that.

For example, if you've been feeling sad lately, rather than asking: "Why am I sad," or "Why am I always so sad," ask, "What would bring me back to joy?"

Of course, you're welcome to ask both! But do ensure you move on to a question that helps guide you forward.

Sometimes your responses might even be questions back to you from your inner guide. This is another way of making you go even deeper by digging up the answers to these questions from within yourself.

For example: "Beautiful soul, what usually brings you joy, and have you been an active participant in the creation of it?"

Maybe you'll realize you've been sitting on the couch moping for so long, or working so hard in your business, you haven't even tried to create some fun and playfulness in your life. Maybe you haven't been taking care of your physical vessel with good sleep, water, nutrition, and exercise, so of course you feel sluggish and tired. Maybe you've been taking on too much responsibility for someone else's happiness, and it has completely drained you of yours.

Maybe somehow you've moved out of alignment in a certain area of your life, and your internal guidance system is giving you a heads up. (More on Soul Alignment coming up later in this book - this is huge!)

Keep asking more questions and then pause in silence while the intuitive, subtle, and loving instinctual reply arises. Trust it and write it down immediately without judgement or filter.

Practice this for between five and fifteen minutes every day and you'll be amazed at what comes through!

Spiritually Clearing Nutrients

Have you ever noticed that when you eat certain foods (maybe things like pasta, bread, red meat, turkey dinners, etc.), it affects the way you feel afterwards? Perhaps you feel heavy, weighted down, tired, foggy minded, and / or lethargic?

Well, the opposite can also be true when we are mindful of how we are nourishing our physical vessels.

Science now proves that the mind and body are connected. The mind and body are also both connected to Source intelligence - channeled to us through our intuition. [1]

When we nourish our physical vessel with high-vibe foods, we keep our channel of communication clear and can more

---

1   Benardis, M. (2013, December 17). How To Make Sure You're Eating High-Vibrational Food. Retrieved from https://www.mindbodygreen.com/0-11996/how-to-make-sure-youre-eating-highvibrational-food.html

easily and effectively connect to our high-vibe inner guide.

Here are a few high-vibe foods you can reach for depending on your needs:

- Citrus fruits = grow in the sun and connect you further to Source.
- Root vegetables = very grounding, they help you to manifest your inspired ideas here on earth.
- Increased water consumption = clarity.

On the other hand, some foods can decrease your connection to your inner guide.

Sugar, processed meats, alcohol, processed foods = increased fogging of the clair senses.

If you are new to connecting to your intuition, reducing these things will provide extra clarity and connection as you develop your new skill.

The cleaner, fresher, and more local and organic your food, the easier it is for you to feel clearer, fresher, and more connected to your Higher Self.

If you're unsure about how certain foods affect you, pay attention to your body and the way you feel after eating those foods.

Each body is different; only you know what's in alignment for your body, and if you pay attention, it will tell you.

Practice

Of course, as with anything in life, the more you practice turning inward, noticing the subtle guidance coming through, and acting on behalf of the insight received, the more easily you will be able to do it without even thinking. Just as learning to drive a stick shift can feel confusing or as though it requires too much effort and thought at first, eventually your body drives the car and changes the gears without you even consciously realizing it anymore.

The same goes for intuition. The more you practice it, the more it will become a natural way of being.

You may reach a point where your intuition guides you on what to say when speaking to anyone, from a saddened friend to an audience of thousands.

- Where it gives you all your best business advice.
- Where it calms you when you feel worried, nervous, or afraid.
- Where it gives you instant insights into who can be trusted in your surroundings, and who to be extra careful with.
- Where you've really learned to tune into it, gaining clarity, guidance, and answers even without meditation or journaling.
- It can be your greatest guide, biggest ally, and wisest mentor.

Here are some tips for practicing and leaning into your intuition:

How to Get An Immediate Yes / No From Your Inner Guide

1. Start with an easy, obvious, "yes" response to a yes / no question that you already know the answer to. For example: "Is my name _____?" Sit quietly for a few moments after answering this question, feeling your body's inner reaction to what you just said. This is what "yes" feels like.

2. Now practice the opposite, an obvious "no" response *to a yes / no question. For example, "Is my name Handker-*chief?" Sit quietly for a few moments after answering this question, feeling your body's inner reaction to what you just said. This is what "no" feels like.

Just as no two people are exactly alike, your inner guidance may feel different within your body than it does within mine or anyone else's. I've commonly found that a "yes" typically feels like a very soft and subtle flutter in the heart / chest space (heart chakra). A shimmer of agreeance, a loving little nod. As subtle as a whisper. So soft, it may take some practice to feel it.

I've also commonly found that a "no" just feels like nothing at all. There's no negative or bad feeling, just no reaction of any kind. No flutter of excitement or loving nod. Just a blank response.

Get to know what this feels like for you within your own body, and then practice making more and more decisions based on this feeling. You can start with small, everyday decisions such as, "Should I brush my teeth today?" "Should I take my vitamins today?" and so on. Work your way up from there.

Keep in mind, depending on your level of connection with your specific intuitive language, if you are clairaudient, you may actually "hear" an inner yes or no. If you are claircognizant, you may have this inner "knowing" of what the right answer is, regardless of the information physically given to you. If you are clairvoyant, you may see an inner picture or movie of yourself going ahead with the decision or not. And if you are clairsentient, you may feel inside your body whether or not something is the right choice for you.

Remember, we are being guided every moment of every day to our highest and best path. The path of least resistance to joy. Like a GPS, your intuition doesn't come and go or stop and start randomly; it's always on and working for you throughout your journey. And it will always redirect you back onto your highest path no matter which seemingly wrong turn you may take.

But you do have free will, so you do not have to listen, tune in, or take action on behalf of these guidances at all. Everything - from what to wear in the morning, to which friend to send some love to, to when to take a job or leave a relationship - is up to you. Your inner guidance system is always there for you, but it's up to you to be open to it and practice connecting with it and following through on its inspired guidances.

Remember to ask for guidance regularly, as our intuition cannot force anything upon us. Our free will means it's up to us to ask for what we want, and it's up to us to do our part and take action based upon our inner guidances in order to co-create the life we desire.

The more we allow our intuition to lead us into new uncharted territories of growth and expansion into joy and new experiences, the more our human ego will kick into high gear and pull out all the stops in an attempt to keep us within our comfort zone where it's nice and "safe."

Now that you know how to tune into your soul's guidance, let's discover how you can follow it to your ultimate bliss, even when your mind is trying everything to stop you.

By far, building trust and taking inspired action in alignment with this trust will be your biggest asset in growing your intuitive connection.
~ Jennifer Jayde

Trust is how your intuition grows in strength and clarity.
~ Jennifer Jayde

2

Freedom from Fear

aka Understanding Ego

CHAPTER 5

What Is Ego, Exactly?

"Ego says, 'Once everything falls into place, then I
will feel peace.' Spirit says, 'once you feel peace,
everything will fall into place.'"
~ Marianne Williamson

In the midst of my biggest battle with ego, I was rarely sleeping through the night. I carried a seemingly permanent ball of stress in my gut every day, and there was so much inner turmoil going on in my head, I wondered if maybe I was going crazy.

At this point, I'd been in mortgage finance for six years, and I just couldn't handle living the same day on repeat, so far out of alignment with my soul, for much longer.

Around this time, I'd also prematurely lost a family member who had been diagnosed with a terminal illness and was given one year to live.

When he passed is when sh*t got real.

I mean really real.

I mean realizing that I was wishing each day would end, the week would end, the year would end - so I could have a small sliver of freedom from my job before I had to go back and face it all over again.

Only my job took up the majority of my waking hours, meaning I was "wishing" the majority of my life would just pass me by.

What an insult to the Source that created me and gave me this gift of life, and to my late family member who would have given anything to live even one more day.

This was so far from what I believe in (*living life to the fullest!*), that I couldn't believe I'd allowed myself to live this way for so long.

What if I went to the doctor and was given a "one year left" diagnosis?

What if I got in my car to go to the grocery store and never made it home?

Would I be happy with the way I'd lived my life? Would I have explored everything my heart longed to experience?

Why was I wasting so much time when I truly had no idea when my time would run out?!

I knew then what I wanted to do - go after my original dream of destination wedding photography.

With this epiphany came an initial high feeling and gut

reaction of *YES!* that filled my whole body.

Followed by a ker-plunk into the abyss of super negative self-talk, Debbie Downer thoughts, and massive, terrifying self-doubt.

Enter, *ego.*

Tell me, have you ever had thoughts like:

- *I'm not pretty enough.*
- *I'm not tall enough.*
- *I'm not thin enough.*
- *I'm not rich enough.*
- *I'm not smart enough.*
- *I'm not educated enough.*
- *I could never do what I dream of doing.*

Or what about...

- *I'll do that when I have more time.*
- *When I have more money, I'll be happy.*
- *It's selfish of me to put myself first.*
- *If I go after my dreams, I'll run out of money and won't be able to keep a roof over my head, pay my bills, or keep food on the table.*
- *What will my parents / spouse / friends / community think if I go after my dreams and then fail?!*
- *There's no way I could ever _____.*
- *If I don't set dreams or goals for myself that are too big, I can avoid disappointment.*
- *It's best to expect the worst so I can be pleasantly surprised if things actually turn out better.*
- *Why do today what I can put off till tomorrow?*

If even one of these phrases sounds familiar to you, you have met your life partner, ego - the opposite of intuition.

The backseat driver.

The inner critic (even inner bully at times).

The monkey on your back.

Ego is like the clichéd annoying mother-in-law. Although she does love you and wants only the best for you, she believes that her advice and opinions are absolute truths and that you are doing yourself a tremendous disservice by not abiding by her every word.

You acknowledge that she only wants the best for you, and you do love her for it, but man, it can get pretty aggravating or defeating to listen to her at times.

You know you can't just cut her out of your life entirely - this person will be a part of your family forever - so instead, you learn how to deal.

If we were to let ego *(or annoying mother-in-laws)* dictate how we live our lives, we would be miserable, and completely out of alignment with our soul's path and inner guidances.

Ego creates strong, believable, fear-based lies (often disguised as logical reasons), based on your own personal, most sensitive buttons, to keep you from moving beyond the safety zone of what's familiar and predictable based on your past experiences.

Its job is to keep you safe. It actually does love you and is not evil, but it will be mean and manipulative in order to serve its purpose. Its tactics can range from simply convincing you to procrastinate on a soul-inspired idea to creating overbearing, overwhelming stress and anxiety, or having you believe you are a terrible human being or that your life is (or the happiness / lives of others are) at risk if you don't heed its "warnings."

Warnings such as:

- You are not smart enough to do this.
- You are not educated enough to do this.
- No one will like you if you speak your mind.
- You will fail if you try something new.
- People will think you're a total joke if and when you fail.

And whatever else it has to make you believe in order to ensure you do not move forward into unknown territory.

So, in the grand scheme of life, why would our soul want to come from a place of pure bliss and joy to inhabit a human body and have to live with something like ego? It's because ego creates contrast. Contrast is how we learn, grow, overcome, and expand. The feeling of overcoming fear (created by ego) is one of the most exhilarating feelings there is in life.

Imagine a time when you faced a fear. Maybe it was asking your boss for a raise. Or holding a snake or spider for the first time. Or starting a new school or new job. Or maybe you're an adventure-seeker like me and went swimming with sharks, bungee jumping, scuba diving, or skydiving.

Remember the fear and panic just before you did it . . . and remember the exhilaration after.

This type of feeling can only be experienced in human

form, thanks to contrast. *Thanks to ego.*

Contrast helps us navigate our path. By knowing what we don't want, we can more easily understand what it is we do want. Humans love the experience of growing, learning, and expanding. A lot of these experiences come from doing things we once thought were impossible. And the reason we once thought it was impossible was because of ego. You see what I mean? Ego is actually serving us, even when it doesn't always feel so good.

The trick is to see ego for what it is, acknowledge it, and move forward beyond it, no matter what it's trying to do to stop you. This can become a much smoother and more enjoyable process than maybe it's been for you before. The first step to overcoming ego's hold on you is being able to see where it's at play in your life . . . where it's been sneaking around and lurking and leading you astray, even without your conscious awareness.

Let's take a deeper look at your own life and burst ego's hold over you now.

Ego asks,
What's in it for me?
Soul asks,
How may I serve?
~ Dr. Wayne Dyer

CHAPTER 6

Recognizing Ego In Your Life And Breaking Free Of Its Pull

"The moment you become aware of the ego in you, it is strictly no longer the ego but just an old, conditioned mind pattern. Ego implies unawareness. Awareness and ego cannot coexist."
~ Eckhart Tolle

What we're about to dig into in this chapter will be eye-opening and may even hit you like a ton of bricks ... so I wanted to give you some guidance on how to navigate what might come up for you as you continue to read. No matter what you've done in your life up until today - whether it was spending years at a job you didn't love, marrying the wrong person, or really anything you knew in your gut wasn't in your best interest - the truth is - yes it was. There is a purpose behind it, there is a master plan in place. *There always is . . .*

The Awakening

One of the very first things I'm being pulled to make you aware of right now is your personal source of motivation behind anything that you do.

For example, let's say you start a business, and you want this business to bring in the big bucks. Like, the BIG, big bucks. So you do whatever it takes to see this vision come to fruition. You hire the business coach. You work tirelessly day and night. You see less of your friends, less of your partner, and spend even less time taking care of yourself. The gym has become a thing of the past. Food? You mean those crackers in the cupboard? Getting dressed is now reserved only for special occasions.

But why?

What does it really boil down to?

What's all this money, drive, and ambition *really for*?

For me, I told myself that it was for my capacity to serve. If I earned more money, I could serve more people.

I could do more things for free for people who really needed it because I would no longer be desperate for money. I could host larger events to serve more lives. And while this is true, there was also a nasty, underlying reason I refused to acknowledge.

I was still running.

Running from fear - created by ego.

I still carried the belief I picked up when I was a kid and I saw my mom suffering from anxiety and panic attacks over the two of us being broke and alone. At four-years-old, I determined that the more money you have, the happier and safer you are.

And as long as I refused to shine a light on this belief, it continued to run the show deep down in my subconscious. It led me to do such things as quit going to the gym, see less and less of my friends and less and less of my spouse, and work more hours in my "dream business" than I ever worked at my nine-to-five.

It led me to become completely out of alignment in all other areas of my life, even though the premise of my business was in alignment with my soul.

In a nutshell, I had attached my sense of happiness, safety, and ultimately my self-worth to the size and success of my business.

Take a look around in your own life, starting with the people you've observed both in person and online.

Can you think of someone who has, from what you can sense, attached their self-worth to how much money they make?

They're in a great mood when they're making lots of money and in a tailspin when they're not?

Can you think of someone who has, from what you can sense, attached their self-worth to a sense of achievement (more education, more courses, more training, more accreditations, etc.)?

For example, they spend more time acquiring more letters and certifications behind their name than they spend actually putting those qualifications to good use?

Can you think of someone who has, from what you can sense, attached their self-worth to adoration from others? Whose actions have an air of attention-seeking for the likes, comments, followers?

While none of these things are wrong (it's not wrong to desire to increase your income, it's not wrong to continue your education or to be well respected by others), when it becomes harmful is when your self-worth cord is attached to them. This makes for one heck of an emotional rollercoaster ride - whether it's in the form of your business, your job, your relationships, your roles as a mother, wife, daughter, etc.

This is just one way that we may be living a life led by ego, rather than from our soul center.

Our soul requires no external validation from the amount of money we make, the material objects we possess, how many social media fans or likes we have, or how much we bend over backwards to please others.

Yup, that one's worth reading again . . .

If this resonates with you in any way, I'm ecstatic to share with you how you can end this draining, emotional roller-coaster ride starting today. But first, let's see what other ego muck could use some clearing, too . . .

Job / Career

If you're in a paid job right now, what would happen if your employer ran into some hard times and wasn't able to pay you for the foreseeable future? Let's also say that you actually already have more money than you need, so whether you get paid or not isn't of any financial concern to you right now.

Would you still keep showing up to your job?

In other words - would you spend time doing what you're doing even if you weren't being paid to do it? It doesn't have to have anything to do with saving the planet or feeding starving children - maybe you're a door greeter at Walmart and you absolutely love smiling at hundreds of people every day - the question is, does it bring out any joy from within you at all? Do you feel like it contributes to your life in a way that is meaningful for you?

If you were to fast forward your life, will you be happy that you spent years of your life doing this work?

If the answer is yes - great!

If the answer is no, what led you to take this job?

Was it inspiration (soul) or desperation (ego)?

Your life's purpose may not have anything to do with your job, career, or business. Perhaps your purpose at this stage in your life is being the very best parent you can be, and that's what really lights you up, but you have to work in order to financially support your family. What we'll talk about more in an upcoming chapter is your Ultimate Purpose, the one that overrides your whole life - joy. So even if your job isn't where you feel your focused life purpose is, you deserve to at least have a job you enjoy.

Let's keep going and clear out as many ego cobwebs as we can!

Personal Health

If you were to rank your priorities based on your last six months of actions, how would your personal health rank?

There's a spectrum here, and I'm curious where you're at on it.

On one end of the spectrum is the absolute lowest possible ranking, where there's been little to no exercise, water, fresh air, regular maintenance, or healthy nourishment.

Then there's the far other end of the spectrum, where you are borderline obsessive about your health and the way you physically look.

On a scale of one to ten, one being the lowest possible ranking and ten being nearing obsessed, where do you rank, in your honest opinion?

Do you enjoy this current reality, or does it need to shift?

What thoughts or beliefs led you to this ranking, if you were being completely honest with yourself?

Soul or ego?

Your soul does not expect you to be in perfect health at all times; it loves you regardless and unconditionally. Your soul is in alignment with love, and its highest desire is for you to treat your body with love in all its forms: kindness, compassion, forgiveness, patience, all without condition. Completely disregarding your health is not in the highest alignment with love, nor is expecting perfection from your body. Ego is on the far ends of the spectrum we described, while soul is right in the middle.

A little added bonus: Next time you begin a new lifestyle change, ask yourself if the motivation is being driven by your soul or by your ego. This will be a great indicator of whether or not the new lifestyle change will stick long-term.

Relationships With Others

Are you a people-pleaser? Do you say "yes" even when you really mean "no?" Do you do things, favors, for others that you wish you didn't have to? Do you use the word "should" quite often? Like "I don't really want to do this, but I guess I should because . . ."

- They'll think I'm a jerk if I say no.
- They did _____ for me, so I owe it to them.
- I'm a good person, so of course I will _____.

When it boils down to it, do your significant other, your friends, and your family members know the truth of who you really are, or do they know the version of you you've allowed them to see - the version you think they'd like?

And if it's the latter, what has kept you from being your full, true self with others?

Ego or soul?

Okay, so if it turns out that some of your life choices and habits have been ego (fear)-based and you feel they are not serving you any longer, where do we go from here?

The first step is already done. **Awareness.** Bringing awareness to something that needs changing is the first, and often most powerful step in creating any kind of change in your life. Without shedding light on what needs to change, we continue sleepwalking through life wondering why we're unhappy or unfulfilled.

So you've got that one done already - woo hoo! (Tip: feel free to go further in-depth with each area of your life, especially ones with which you are currently unhappy).

The second step is to bring this awareness into your everyday life and **start making different choices** than you have made before.

For example, if you were about to people-please and say "yes" when you really meant "no," start practicing the subtle art of saying no - with class, but without explanation or excuse. A simple "As much as I'd love to help, I'm not available right now" is a great example of how to do this.

The third step is repeating your new choices until they become a habit. A habit is something that happens on autopilot so you no longer even think about it consciously. It's your new natural way of being.

Ahhh . . . no more self-defeating thoughts, habits, or rituals - imagine! It's possible, and you can start today . . .

Our soul requires no external
validation from the amount
of money we make,
The material objects we possess,
How many social media fans
or likes we have,
Or how much we bend over
backwards to please others.
~ Jennifer Jayde

CHAPTER 7

Using Ego to Your Advantage

"The ego promotes turmoil because it wants to substantiate your separatness from everyone, including God. It will push you in the direction of judgment and comparison, and cause you to insist on being right and best. You know your highest self by listening to the voice that only wants you to be at peace."
~ Dr. Wayne Dyer

When I was making the leap from my nine-to-five to my first full-time dream business, there really was one thing that pushed me over the edge from staying in the safe and familiar to taking a leap of faith and seeing what would be possible as a destination wedding photographer.

And it was actually . . . *fear.*

Where once my fear of failure had kept me still, stuck, and stagnant, I realized I had another fear even greater - *the fear of regret on my deathbed.*

This fear rose to the surface after the loss of my loved one. He was just over a decade older than me, had two little girls aged six and eight, and was not ready to leave his family behind. He fought tooth and nail to live for even one more day.

And I couldn't help but internalize this. *What if this happened to me one day? What if I just kept humming along feeling moderately happy (but not really), until one day I'm told it will all be over within a year? Or what if I get in a car accident tomorrow? Will I be happy with the way that I lived my life . . . or was I just existing . . . passing time, waiting for the weekend to come? Waiting for my one or two-week holiday every year?*

I attached myself to *this* fear instead, and *that is* what got me through leaving my nine-to-five behind for good.

Any time the creeping sensations came in that maybe I had lost my mind and really shouldn't be giving up my career in finance, I fast-forwarded my life, pictured myself on my deathbed (morbid maybe, but extremely clarifying for me), and asked that version of me if she would regret not finding out what could've been. And when it was a "yes," I moved forward despite the limiting inner critic beliefs. I felt the fear, *and did it anyway.*

Another time ego has served me is (funny enough) in the gym.

I remember being on a treadmill as part of a circuit training program I was doing. I'm pretty good with trying to improve each time by slightly increasing the speed or the incline, but this particular day, a girl next to me made me feel like I was a geriatric exerciser! So what did I do? Pumped up the speed, of course!

Because I was aware of how ego works by this time, in that moment, I was able to detach my self-worth and value from whether or not I could compete with this girl and go as fast (or faster) than her. I instead used my ego to my advantage, to be inspired and push myself a little further than I had been before.

Lo and behold, I was actually able to run faster and farther than I had ever allowed myself to previously believe!

It turns out, my ego had been holding me back in one way - telling me I could only go so fast. But I could actually flip that and use ego to convince me to go a little faster than I previously believed I could!

The key here is awareness.

Be aware of when ego is holding you back, and instead choose to make a new decision, even if at first it involves using ego to encourage you to move forward.

When it's ego telling you to compete with others in any way, detaching from comparison with others, detaching your self-worth from the outcome (more on this coming up!), and instead using ego as inspiration to push yourself beyond your comfort zone in a loving way is what will serve your growth. Get curious about what's possible, and go for it without any attachment to the outcome!

What about you? Have you ever worked out with a personal trainer, for example, or with a friend, and they encouraged you to do something you didn't think you could? Lifting a heavier weight or doing a certain number of pushups?

The first thing you might hear in your mind is *I can't do this.*

But when you have someone there rooting for you, telling you over and over and over again that you can - how often do you surprise yourself and find that you can actually do more than your ego would've allowed you to believe?

Disclaimer - this is not permission to ignore your body's warning signs and push yourself into injury. There is a difference between your head telling you *I can't do that* in a negative way and your body telling you that it's reached its present limits. Rather, this is an invitation to stretch yourself beyond what's comfortable, a little more, and a little more, like you would in a yoga practice.

Ultimately, the goal is to no longer make any kind of fear / ego-based decisions at all. But if this serves you in a transitional phase and helps you gain momentum until then, feel free to use it!

When you've practiced observing ego at play in your mind and in your life, when you've learned that you no longer need to take orders from your ego or be slowed down by it, or even believe the lies it's feeding you, you then begin tuning in to the deeper, softer, more subtle part of you - your soul. This part of you will always guide you in a loving way.

Don't let a fear that 99%
of the time won't even happen,
rule 99% of your life.
~ Jennifer Jayde

CHAPTER 8

Soul Freedom - Detaching From The Outcome And Letting Go Of The How

"When the ego dies, the soul awakes."
~ Mahatma Gandhi

Detaching From The Outcome

The art of detaching from the outcome is a total game changer in life and business. This is the fast-tracked path to everything you truly wanted, with as much ease, joy, and flow as there could possibly be . . .

I still remember the feeling as if it were happening now. My palms would be sweating, hands subtly shaking, knees trembling. I would feel like someone cranked the heat in the room to a million degrees, and hoped my sweat wasn't visible anywhere on my body.

Finally, like clockwork, every Tuesday morning, the manager at the real estate office would call my name to speak about mortgage rates, economic forecasts for financing, and tips or special offers we had going on at my mortgage office.

I was massively intimidated and uncomfortable because:

- At twenty-two-years-old, I barely knew what I was talking about in a room full of mostly middle-aged men;
- I didn't like speaking in front of crowds AT ALL; and
- I was petrified of an unwelcomed outcome - someone would ask me a question that I would know nothing about and call me out for the fraud that I actually felt like inside.

And yet, I went back every. single. week. Tuesday, after Tuesday, after Tuesday.

And after a while, I finally just got so exhausted from giving so many f*cks that I just let them all go. *Screw it,* I thought to myself and I just started enjoying it. I started smiling, cracking jokes, being myself. I let go of all the fears I was holding on to so tightly because it was exhausting, and really didn't serve me at all to be worried so much.

When I relaxed and let go, I could sense that the realtors also warmed up to me and were relaxed around me. They started chatting with me more, welcoming me to come sit with them, and even referring me to clients. Ahhhh . . . big exhale.

For this, I thank three things:

1. Finally getting so sick and tired of being so worried about what other people think that I just couldn't carry the burden anymore. I let it go.

2. Repetition. I really didn't have a say in the matter of whether or not I went every Tuesday to the real estate meeting; the owner of our office didn't leave it up to me. After repeating something so many times, I finally relaxed and found my own groove.

3. Time. Everyone was a beginner once. *The only difference is consistenc...y. (Damn, I really wanted that to rhyme . . .)*

Another opportunity to learn how to detach from the outcome came with photographing weddings. In the beginning, I was super *attached to a favorable outcome* and would take it personally if I met with a couple interested in hiring me for their wedding photography and then never heard from them again.

Luckily, I had a mentor who told me to keep looking forward, to welcome the next opportunity to meet more couples, and that the Universe was always looking out for me. If one couple didn't hire me, it was because we weren't a good fit, and I just needed to trust that. Now I had space for the couple that would be the right fit. And sometimes I'd take it one step further and thank the Universe for helping me dodge a bullet - perhaps a nightmare bride! Likely not always true, but it helped me move on nonetheless.

But I really learned the art of detaching myself from the outcome when I started my online coaching business.

I decided to start with one-on-one private coaching packages, and offered a complimentary clarity call so my potential client could get a feel for me and decide whether or not to hire me as their coach.

I found myself right back in the place I was when I first started to speak at the real estate meetings or to book wedding photography clients. I was new to coaching so I felt like a fraud; I was insecure about myself and my services, and if someone chose not to work with me, I took it personally and became saddened and filled with even more self-doubt.

Thankfully, it didn't take me long to realize I had been here before and that it did not serve me to give so many f*cks. I also remembered that I would feel more comfortable with time and repetition.

Another thing - I remembered *(and attached instead to)* WHY I was super inspired to become a coach in the first place. I remembered the invaluable shifts it created for me in my own life, and how excited I was to facilitate these same life-changing shifts for others.

I became excited instead of insecure.

Whenever someone chose not to work with me, I thanked the Universe for saving me from a client who wasn't a good match and for keeping my calendar open for the amazing client who is about to hire me. "There's more where that came from," I would silently say to myself and carry on with my day.

And soon I realized, the less I worried about the outcome, the more people wanted to hire me.

The desperation I was unconsciously giving off was replaced with a dash of "you need me more than I need you" *(in a good way, of course!).* I went from giving off that stereotypical desperate car salesman vibe to being a magnet for those looking to transform their life from unhappy and misaligned to fulfilled and free full-time.

What about you, my friend?

Is there somewhere in your life you've been carrying around thoughts of self-doubt or perhaps caring a little too much about what other people think - in your work, your relationship, your friendships, your body?

Do these thoughts affect the way you feel - maybe bringing you down, allowing sadness in, or causing you to second-guess yourself and what you're capable of?

What would it feel like to just say the two magic words that worked so well for me - Screw it *(or whatever colorful words you choose!)* - and just go for it?

Everything is always turning out in your favor, whether or not it's in the way you'd expected or wanted it to.

If people align with your vision, say yes, come along for the ride, hire you, agree with you, commend you, compliment you - great! But even if they don't, thank the Universe for the experience and for saving the space for something (or someone) better to come along.

Detaching From The "How"

I was about six years old in our little basement suite with my mom, and one morning she overheard me singing one of my dad's *(the rock'n'roller I saw on weekends)* favorite songs . . .

"Raise a little how, raise a little how, raise a little how!!!" (Which was actually a song called *Raise a Little Hell* by Trooper)

I thought I had the lyrics right, and so did she, and gave me hell for singing "how" . . .

Detaching from the "how" is just as significant a game-changer in life as detaching from outcome.

Here's the difference:

Detaching from the Outcome - Doing whatever inspired action is aligned with an outcome you desire but not attaching your sense of self-worth, value, or capabilities on whatever that outcome happens to be.

Detaching from the "How" - Getting clear on *how* you want your life and business to *feel* (starting with the end goal in mind), but not dictating (or waiting around until you know) every single step in order to get the whole way there. Instead, following the breadcrumbs of inspired ideas, connections, actions, etc. that the Universe leaves for you, one step at a time. Taking action on these, trusting each step, even before you can see the next. *This* is how you create from a place of flow, your path of least resistance. When you instead try to force the *how* in a way your ego / head has determined is correct, you can find yourself taking quite a long and exhausting detour.

At sixteen-years-old, I was pissed. Pissed that I didn't know what I was going to do with my life, what courses I should be taking as prerequisites for college, what I should be taking in college, and what career path to follow. I was super driven and ambitious (running from my childhood fear of lack and scarcity, little did I know at the time), and I just wanted to know HOW I was going to be rich and successful so I never had to worry about money the way I saw my mother worrying when I was a child.

Someone asked me, "Well, what do you know you want?"

{{{Great question!!!}}}

This is exactly what I replied . . .

"I don't know what I wanna do, but I know I'm not gonna do it for anyone else. I want to be my own boss, make my own hours, go on vacation without asking permission, and have absolutely no ceiling on how much money I can make . . ."

What I didn't say, but also knew, was that I was too afraid to take on the risk of having my own business and didn't have any money or any CLUE on how to do that. Wasn't there some way I could have the best of both worlds?

Looking back, I can see clearly now that the Universe actually did provide me everything I asked for, because I did not force the how. (I couldn't force the how back then even if I'd tried, simply because I had zero clue how that could ever be possible).

Right after graduation, still having no clue what I was going to do with my life and feeling lost, I went travelling. I lived in London, England for a short while with two girlfriends and worked at a Penderel's Oak Pub called JD Wetherspoon's and at a concert venue called Shepherd's Bush Empire. Clearly not as my own boss, not making my own hours, and with a defined income ceiling.

After coming home to Canada and looking for a job, my mildly depressed teenaged self was offered a job through a friend-of-a-friend in finance.

Through a chain of events from there, I took my license to become a mortgage broker.

And as a 100% commission-based mortgage broker, I:

- Was my own boss, aside from the owner of the company who gave me free reign to create my income as I pleased;
- Made my own hours;
- Went on vacation without having to ask permission;
- Had no ceiling on the amount of income I could make; and
- Had my office, laptop, and business cards paid for by the company.

I didn't realize it then, but the Universe had led me, breadcrumb after breadcrumb, into exactly all that I had asked for.

When you begin practicing the art of detaching from the outcome *and* the *how*, your life will become far lighter, freer, and filled with more ease and flow than perhaps it's ever been.

As a recovering type-A-perfectionist-control-freak who learned the value of - and adopted - this practice, I can promise you this: being in flow with the Universe and trusting its subtle guidances will always be your path of least resistance to anything and everything you desire.

When your next steps are unclear,
run towards your fear.
~ Jennifer Jayde

3

Awakening Your Spiritual Energy

CHAPTER 9

Why Am I Sad?

*"Think of your emotions as cups in your chest.
They can only fill up so much before they start to
overflow out of you."*
~ Jennifer Jayde

Have you ever gone through periods of your life when you feel sad yet cannot seem to put your finger on how it all started - or even what will actually make you feel better?

Maybe you turn to food, chocolate, ice cream, wine, shopping, or hiding in your house Netflix'in it up on your couch until the unhappiness hopefully subsides...

And what about your relationship with anger?

What do you do when someone hurts your feelings, angers or upsets you? Anything?

What do you do with the pent-up energy from the asshole who was driving below the speed limit when you were running late for work or picking up your kids or rushing to get to your fitness class?

What about the emotions you feel after attending a stressful family dinner or event, or when a friend said something hurtful unintentionally? What happens when your beloved totally disregarded how hard you worked today or the nice things you did?

What do you do with that? If you're anything like I was . . . nothing.

I would do nothing but try to brush it off, see the silver lining, see the positive, see the lesson, and move forward. But unfortunately, it doesn't work that way. Emotional energy cannot be created or destroyed by simply ignoring it.

My positive outward appearance and focus even fooled me for a time, until I began to grow increasingly sad with no idea of how it had crept up on me. This sadness even led me to feeling extremely fatigued physically, to the point when I would sleep more and more hours a night and still feel like I needed a nap by the late morning. I was starting to worry there was something seriously wrong with my health, like a thyroid issue or worse.

I was just about to set up an appointment with my doctor when yet another teaching came as a gift from the Universe. It was this...

Whether we identify with being an "angry" person or not, we're all human, and thus we all experience the range of human emotions, including anger. Little daggers throughout the day that we "positive" people like to brush under the rug while we only look for the bright side. And while yes, it is a great practice to continually turn your focus, attention, and energy to the positives and lessons, this doesn't dispel the need to release the negative emotions that build up over time.

Think of your emotions as cups in your chest. They can only fill up so much before they start to overflow out of you.

So if you are, say, uncomfortable with releasing anger, anger will actually pour out into a cup that you are more willing to release - such as sadness (and it may very likely also show up as being snippy with those closest to us - our kids, mom, spouse, sibling, etc . . .).

And there we have it - we find ourselves sad, unhappy, perhaps even crying - for no real reason. We can't understand where this sadness is coming from, or how to get rid of it.

Because it was never sadness to begin with.

So what do we do? Keep reading . . .

For me, I've never been one to get openly angry or confrontational with people. So I wasn't about to start causing scenes in grocery store lineups every time I got annoyed with someone asking for a price check (but seriously, am I the only one this drives wild?!), nor was I about to have road rage on the retiree who should have given up his license long ago - and I wouldn't ask that of you either.

So how can we empty the anger cup (or sadness cup or whichever cup you've been neglecting to release) without dumping our emotions all over people, especially at truly inappropriate times?

I'm glad you asked! :)

Take the energy of this emotion and use it for something else - intentionally.

For example, go for a run. Set the intention that with every step, every breath, you are letting go and releasing any feeling or thought that no longer serves you. Or go to a kickboxing class. With every punch and kick, you release more and more of anything that does not serve you.

Or go for a drive and yell-sing your favorite uplifting songs.

Or punch a pillow and scream into it until you start laughing.

Smash some thrift shop plates in your garage.

Go to the gym (remember to set your intention first, and be safe during your workout). Try a new fitness class.

Journal every angry thought until you are no longer carrying the weight of it inside.

Yell inside your garage or car.

Talk it out with a trusted best friend who gets that their only job is to listen and allow you to vent.

Cry, if you feel like crying. It can be in the shower, or wherever you feel safe to truly let the tears flow.

Write an angry letter with all of your truest and deepest angry thoughts. You are not a bad person because you are angry! You are human! Let it go. Let it out. Free yourself of this burden. And then burn it if you desire to. Breathing techniques (find some online on Youtube, Gaia.com, MindBodyGreen.com, Yoga Journal!).

Whatever you choose - do it with the intention of letting go. Be consistent with your practice, and notice your energy and mood soar!

Journal Exercise

Grab a paper and pen and work through the questions below. Allow your answers to come from the deepest part of your soul, and be free of judgement as your answers flow freely onto the page. In order to heal, we must be willing to acknowledge and release what no longer serves us.

What emotional cup have you been neglecting the most?

How has this been showing up in your life?

How has this been affecting you? How has this been affecting the people around you?

What would it be like to let that go? What would that mean for you, and how would it feel?

How would it affect your life (and your dreams) to let this go regularly?

How would it affect the people around you?

On a scale of one to ten, how committed are you to this

new way of being? Why?

Starting today, what are three possible ways you could start releasing any pent-up emotion?

How long and how regularly will you commit to the practice to see if it works for you?

When will you start?

Whatever you hold in your mind on a consistent basis is exactly what you will experience in your life.
~ Tony Robbins

People will feel
your energy louder
than they will
hear your words.
~ Jennifer Jayde

CHAPTER 10

How To Cleanse, Protect, And Uplift Your Energy

*"If you want to find the secrets of the Universe,
think in terms of energy, frequency and vibration."*
~ Nikola Tesla

Aside from carrying around stuck, negative emotion, we often experience another powerful energy drainer.

At one point in my life, I found myself in a repeated pattern of going to the mall for an hour or two and coming home feeling completely drained and exhausted, like I'd just run a marathon. I got to thinking . . . *You know, walking at a snail's pace around a mall shouldn't really be this physically exhausting, Jen . . .*

Then I'd notice it again after attending a family gathering.

And again, after going to the grocery store and other populated places.

Finally, I got curious enough to welcome the "teacher" into my life for this lesson.

I was at an appointment with a natural practitioner who'd just gotten back from a spiritual retreat. She told me all about shielding.

AND IT CHANGED MY LIFE.

Chances are, if you notice a shift in your energy or emotions with no rational explanation (other than what we learned earlier in this book), there is a good chance you are an Empath and / or Clairsentient to some degree.

Empath - Someone who feels the pain and emotion of others and often absorbs it as their own if they are not careful or unaware. Tip: If you're curious as to whether or not you may be an Empath, head to *jenniferjayde.com/theawakeningbook* for a quick reference guide.

Clairsentient - Clear sensing, the ability to feel the present, past, or future physical and emotional states of others, without the use of the normal five senses. People who are clairsentient are able to retrieve information from houses, public buildings, and outside areas, as well as from other people.

Now it's time I show you how you reclaim your energy.

There are many different ways to clear energies that are bogging you down, whether they are coming from your own personal emotions and experiences or someone else's.

I started with a morning recording that I would listen to once I was out of bed and just waking up for the day.

Here's how you can create your own powerful morning energy cleanser, replenisher, and protector . . .

Morning Ritual Recording

Step #1

Find or create a daily morning ritual (five to seven minutes) that includes:

- Cleansing the old energy accumulated from yesterday's surroundings, thoughts, and feelings, or even from uncomfortable dreams from last night. Marianne Williamson says cleansing yesterday's energy is even more important than cleansing yesterday's dirt![2]
- Grounding yourself and connecting yourself to Source (the higher power of your understanding).
- Opening up your chakras (energy centers).
- Protecting / shielding yourself from low-vibe energy or energy drainers all day.

(Psssst - If you like, you can use mine here: jenniferjayde.com/theawakeningbook)

Step #2

Before entering into any particularly draining situations (such

---

2   MARIANNE WILLIAMSON INTERVIEW: RECLAIMING THE POWER OF THE FEMI-NINE. (2015, October 25). Retrieved from https://www.the-numinous.com/2015/10/25/marianne-williamson-interview/

as the mall, grocery stores, family gatherings, work, bank, doctor's office, etc.), set a fresh shield or intention before walking in. This can be simply a three-second silent visualization or intention.

Here are a few examples to get you started...

- Imagine a fresh gold or white bubble surrounding you and protecting you. High-vibes / frequency / love flow in and out, but   anything of a negative / lower frequency can only be repelled.
- Imagine a shield of mirrors facing outward from you, repelling all energy that does not serve you.
- Step into a sleeping bag-like cocoon and zip it up from head to toe.
- Say silently to yourself, "I enter this place with only my own energy and feelings, and I will leave with all my own energy and feelings."

Stay consistent with this practice - and watch as negative things no longer affect you nearly as much as they once did.

Eventually, I started incorporating a visualization into my morning ritual this took about another ten or fifteen seconds in total. These visualizations can really be anything you want, as long as they make you *feel* the release of what no longer serves you.

Visualizations

Example 1: Cutting The Cords

Cutting cords with someone you love does not diminish your love, connection, or bond - it simply separates you from their baggage, stories, energy, beliefs, drama, and perceptions that no longer serve you.

Yes, you still love them, yes, they still love you, and yes, you are still connected and see each other as often as feels good. But no, you do not have to carry their energetic weight anymore.

Step #1

Imagine you are surrounded by those who influence you the most, even those who may potentially drain you, whether they mean to or not. This could be parents, family, friends, co-workers, exes, clients, etc. Now imagine that you have a cord running from you to them.

Step #2

Envision a pair of weedwackers or giant scissors or whatever you choose, and imagine the cord being cut between the two of you. You are freeing this person to take their power back, and you are freeing yourself to keep your own.

You are doing both of you a service.

You can make any variation of this cord-cutting visual that you like. Maybe you turn it into "unplugging" the cord, or whatever else feels good and empowering to you, for both of you.

Example 2: Awakening To Your Giant Power

Imagine yourself laying down in a big open field. You are

tied down to this field by your hands, arms, chest, feet, and legs. You've just been laying there because you didn't see the point in trying to get up.

But in this moment, you decide to own your power, and you slowly rise and sit up.

Surprisingly, it comes easily to you. The binds that were holding you down really were no stronger than strands of hair. They snap in half without any strain or effort at all.
You realize if you can sit up, you can stand up.

And you do.

You are stronger and larger than life.

The binds fall to the ground, and you're walking gracefully and powerfully away from all the worries, beliefs, and doubts you thought could hold you down . . .

And when you learn how to do this (simply and easily) for yourself, you will begin to feel a million times lighter than you did before.

Happier, even.

Energized. Vivacious.

And ready to flow with life, whatever it may bring.

There simply is not enough action
in the world to compensate
for the misalignment of energy.
But when you care about how you
feel and you tend to your
vibrational balance first,
Then you experience what feels like
a cooperative Universe that seems to
open doors for you everywhere.
~ Abraham Hicks

CHAPTER 11

Getting Into Vibrational Alignment

(How to Manifest Everything You've Ever Wanted)

"The law of attraction is most understood when you see yourself as a magnet getting more and more of the way you feel."
~ Abraham Hicks

Have you ever had moments when you were stricken with panic? Like maybe the tax bill for this year is a lot more than you were expecting, or you accidentally dented another car, or a friend is upset / angry over something you did?

Maybe you're worried about your finances, your relationship, your business, or your health?

I've faced these too, and I completely understand how over-whelming the worry, stress, and fear can be.

I used to think that I was supposed to immediately focus

on the positive. Ignore what was happening before my very eyes and think about all the good in my life instead. But while focusing on gratitude and appreciation is absolutely powerful, it doesn't erase the fact that the tax bill is still massive, or that your friend is still angry with you, or the sting of realizing you no longer fit into your favorite pair of jeans, or a negative health diagnosis.

So what do we do?

In moments of panic, worry, fear, or stress - rather than trying to trick yourself into being happy or ignoring the emotional energy building up inside of you, find a way to go back into neutral.

You don't have to go from panic-stricken to happy and positive.

Just find a way to exhale. Relax. Come to a place where your heart slows down a bit and you're breathing a bit easier.

This can be through:

- Coming back to this present moment. You're alive and breathing. This means there is another opportunity to reclaim your power and get through this.
- Remembering that you've previously faced hard times and struggles in different forms, and you made it through. You made it through then, and you will make it through now.
- Understanding this will pass. It feels fresh and big right now, but eventually it will be old news, too.
- Know the Universe never gives you more than you can handle, trust that whatever is happening to you is happening for you. You are a diamond being shaped

and refined through pressure, and you will come out better on the other side of this.
- Trust.

Some other methods for rising out of stress could be meditating, going for a walk outside, going for a drive, journalling, turning on some uplifting music, connecting with a trusted friend, taking a relaxing bath, listening to an inspiring podcast or audiobook, watching someone uplifting on Youtube, or reading a soul-refreshing book.

Keeping the intention to relax and rise into neutral - not to spend this time overthinking, overanalyzing, or trying to find a solution to your problem.

Once you're in a state of a more relaxed, stable presence, you've found your way back to neutral. Congrats!

And when you're ready, it's time to start moving back up the emotional scale.

It's said that different emotional states of being emit varying levels of measurable frequency.[3]

For example, willingness carries a higher vibration than neutrality.

Acceptance carries a higher vibration than willingness, and optimism carries a higher vibration than acceptance.

---

3   Thompson, C. (2012, January). The Map of Consciousness - Hawkins' Scale. Stankov's Universal Law Press. Retrieved from http://www.stankovuniversallaw.com/2012/01/the-map-of-consciousness-hawkins-scale/.

Then we rise even further into positive expectation, followed by passion, then love, joy, and appreciation - with the very top of the scale being enlightenment.

It is from these states closer to enlightenment that we can actually process with more ease and effectiveness what is going on in our life, and even begin to receive clear inner guidance on the best possible solution / way to move forward.

Have you experienced this before? You received the news of something unfavorable - be it in your finances, relationship, business, health, or otherwise - and it just seemed so big. It was all you could see, all you could think about - and you didn't know what to do about it?

How could you solve it? So you rummaged your brain searching for answers, you were stressed, worried, maybe even lost sleep.

And when you finally exhausted yourself from caring so much and almost gave up . . . bam!

Suddenly it was like the clouds parted, and one by one, things seemed to start getting better.

This was, in part at least, because you naturally found your way back to neutrality (through self-exhaustion). And from there, you chose to start noticing here and there, the things that were working out better for you.

And this led to momentum and more and more things working out for you. Your vibration raised further, and so you attracted similar energy into your reality.

The higher you raise your vibration, the more you welcome

ideas, experiences, people, income, opportunities, and the like that match your vibration into your experience.

This is great news, friend!

What this means is that at any given moment, you can choose to shift your energy. You can choose to change the momentum of your reality.

It starts with your thoughts and then moves out into your emotional energy, and the Universe responds to your energy with like energy (manifesting in the form of people, experiences, ideas, guidances, income, good health, etc., in your reality).

Many people ask why their thoughts don't just manifest immediately. "I want more money, Jen! So where is it?"

If you've ever wondered this, here is a super important thing to note: The Universe is not responding to your words or wish lists. It does not speak language, it responds to (mirrors might be a better word!) your energy, your vibration. So if your words "I want more money" are carrying the feeling of "I don't have enough money" - the Universe will respond to the feeling of not having enough money - not the words or the wish list.

"Doesn't the Universe know I want more money? Why would it continue to give me something (lack of money) it knows I don't want?"

The Universe does not discriminate among your thoughts, it doesn't pick and choose for you what you mean or don't mean to put into your vibration - it simply says yes to *all* of it. Whether it is what you want or not. It loves you so much, it *always* says yes! So be sure you're asking for what you do want by aligning your vibration with that - rather than aligning your thoughts (and therefore your vibration) with what you don't want.

"But Jen, I have no money, not enough anyway. So how do I get on the vibration of having lots of money, if I don't?"

Ah yes! This is where most people get confused. Here's the key, I wish every single person on the planet could know and understand this: You don't have to try and convince yourself you're already rich. You don't have to pretend or feel like you're lying to yourself. Instead, understand the feeling you'll have when you do have more money (engulf yourself in the feeling of joy, happiness, freedom, etc.) and start noticing where you experience that feeling already in your life today.

Did you have the freedom to go outside on your lunch break today? Do you have the freedom to do whatever you want, for even one hour this weekend? Do you have the joy of having an amazing partner or close friend in your life?

Focus on the *feelings* you want to experience more of - because as we've learned, what you focus on, expands.

Let this sink in a bit more . . .

What you focus on expands.

And you can most definitely use this to manifest / create more and more of what you truly do desire in your life.

Because the bottom line is, it's truly not the things, the experiences, or even the money that you want. It's what you believe you will feel once you have them.

So the million dollar trick here is to focus on what your deep desired emotions truly are.

And once you've narrowed it down to your top two or three, you can start to focus on these in your day-to-day experiences, because - say it with me - "What you focus on expands."

Here are some ways you can get to the bottom of why you desire what you desire - your *true* and deepest desired feelings:

- Have you ever made a vision board? Take a look at it and ask yourself how you will feel when you have each thing on the board. Why did you choose to put a yacht, a trip, a ripped bod, or a new car on there? How do you think each of those things would make you feel once you have them? (Note: even if you haven't made a vision board before, you can still use this exercise by thinking about what you would put on a vision board. Or, check out your Pinterest boards if you have them!)

- Write down a list of your top twenty-five to fifty words to describe how you'd ultimately love to feel each morning when you wake up. Once done, start crossing out all of the synonyms until you narrow right down to the top two or three most highly desired feelings.

- Think of things that are bogging you down right now (but not for too long, of course!). Are you the most stressed about money? Relationships? Your body? Your business? Then acknowledge them and flip the script. By knowing what you don't want, you can gain clarity on what you do want. Perhaps you desire to feel prosperous (instead of broke), free (instead of trapped), and fulfilled (instead of bored).

Here are some of the most common, deepest desired feelings I've observed with the ladies in my online programs (circle / write down the ones you desire the most):

Fulfilled   Purposeful

Abundant   Free   Passionate

Inspired   Aligned   Joyful   Powerful

Limitless   Infinite

Happy   Peaceful   Ease

Expansive   Open

Rich   Unbound   Adventurous   Playful

Creative   Spacious   Radiant

Rising   Empowered

In-Spirit   Grateful   Authentic

One note: Ensure your top two or three deeply desired feelings consist of feelings you yourself can be responsible for creating. For example, choosing the word "loved" insinuates getting other people to love you or hoping they will show signs that they do. Instead, choose a more self-empowered feeling, such as Unconditional Self-Love, Authentic, or Soul-Aligned.

Once you have your top two or three most deeply rooted desired emotions, it's time to start the practice of shifting your daily focus toward feeling this way as much, and as often, as possible.

So stop staring at vision boards and wishing to have a massive yacht one day, but also holding the silent thought of "Pfft, yeah right." This stifles your momentum and holds you back from getting into the same frequency as a yacht owner (for example). Instead, you can move toward this desired reality by creating momentum in that direction, starting today.

More specifically, if a yacht would make you feel rich or free - start noticing *where* in your life do you feel this type of abundance already. Do you have an abundance of fresh water as soon as you turn on your tap? An abundance of fresh air when you step outside? An abundance of love from friends, family, or pets? An abundance of clothes in your closet to last you at least a week? An abundance of shoes so that your feet never touch a wet, rainy sidewalk? An abundance of entertainment through your internet connection? As you go through your day each day, simply notice where you are experiencing abundance - especially in ways you may have been overlooking and taking for granted.

Remember, what you focus on expands.

Want to move this momentum even faster?

Start practicing gratitude for all the ways you are abundant already. Thank the Universe for every dollar in your bank account, even if your bank balance is little or even non existent (for now). Instead of focusing on lack and wishing you had more, start expressing appreciation for what you do have.

Express silent gratitude to the Universe every time you spot a penny on the ground by picking it up and saying thank you! Even if only in your mind.

Express silent gratitude to the Universe every time you go to the cash register at the grocery store and something was on sale, the bill was cheaper than you thought it'd be, or the cashier rings through a coupon you didn't have.

And this is just for the deep desired feeling of abundance.

If you desire to feel free - where in your life do you experience freedom already?

- Do you have the freedom to wear whatever you want?
- Do you have the freedom to say how you feel?
- Do you have the freedom to find another job and quit this one if you wanted to?
- Do you have the freedom to go on vacation?
- Do you have the freedom to spend your money as you choose?
- Do you have the freedom to choose what food you'll eat?
- Do you have the freedom to exercise?
- Do you have the freedom to smile, to laugh, to sing, to dance?
- Do you have the freedom to go outside?
- Do you have the freedom to walk?
- Do you have the freedom to breathe?
- Do you have the freedom to feed, bathe, and take care of yourself?
- Do you have the freedom to learn about almost anything you want to online?
- Do you have the freedom to connect with friends and family who live out of town?
- Do you have the freedom to meet up with friends and / or create new ones?
- Do you have the freedom to choose, every day, every moment, your thoughts, and therefore the way you feel?

I once thought I could never have a negative thought or be sad or stressed. I once thought I had to try and somehow leap from worried and overwhelmed to happy-happy, positive-positive - and it just created more stress.

Understand that all we really need to do is get ourselves to neutral, relax - and then, and only then, work our way up the emotional scale. This is so, so much easier, and faster, than what I was trying to do before (which felt more like banging my head against a wall trying to convince myself to just be happy).

And once I started practicing intentionally moving in the direction of my deepest desired feelings, each day my momentum train started moving a little faster, and a little faster - until things were moving so swiftly in alignment with my desires, even I was surprised.

And before long, I was beginning to attract all the things that were once on my vision board with ease. I was in vibrational alignment with them, and they flowed to me. This was not without action, of course - but it was through inspired action that was given to me as I became more and more in alignment with what I desired.

With the vibration I was focusing on . . .

And now, sister, it's your turn.

Vibrational Momentum Tip:

Bring your awareness back to your top two or three deeply desired feelings / vibrations as much as possible throughout the day. You can do this through:

- Setting reminders in your phone alerts;
- Making an intention bracelet (anything from a rubber band to a wrap bracelet with chimes);
- Writing your desired feelings on post-it notes and placing them where you will often see them (bathroom mirror, workspace, car dashboard, etc.).

Whatever you hold in your mind
on a consistent basis is
exactly what
you will experience in your life.
~ Tony Robbins

What you focus on expands.
~ Jennifer Jayde

4

Awakening Your Purpose

CHAPTER 12

What is Purpose - And What Does It Feel Like?

"The basis of life is freedom. The purpose of life is joy.
The result of life is expansion."
~ Abraham Hicks

Recently, I began viewing purpose with even greater clarity than ever before.

Not too long ago, the word "purpose" never even entered my vocabulary. I was working my job as a mortgage broker, feeling like a fish trying to swim upstream - in a stream where I didn't even belong.

Then, the depleting daze of unfulfillment and the soul-shaking awakening from a loss in my family created the perfect storm for me to find my way out of the collective hypnosis and into my childhood dream (of traveling and taking photos for a living). It was then that I began using the word "passion" for the first time in my life.

But, unknowingly, I still wasn't using the word "purpose."

It wasn't until I started living my life in the service of uplifting those around me that I began to feel any sort of semblance of what purpose really was. What living a meaningful life actually felt like, for me.

Living my passion was fun (exhilarating, even!) for a while, but it was something I was doing simply for me. Because I wanted to, and I enjoyed it. And that is completely okay (and encouraged).

But after a while, doing something just for myself no longer filled up my soul cup.

I personally craved to be uplifting, empowering, and wanted to inspire others to live their passions, their dreams, and their purposes, too.

And that's when I started coaching, teaching, and sharing the messages I've learned along the way.

This has given me the deepest sense of purpose, fulfillment, and joy I've ever known.

Abraham Hicks says, *"The basis of life is freedom. The purpose of life is joy. The result of life is expansion . . . "*

Have you been wondering what your purpose is, sister?

I'm about to share it with you, but brace yourself. It may not be the clouds parting, earth-shaking, God-light-beaming-down-on-you that you may have imagined this epiphany to be. Actually, it's the same as when you discover your most dominant intuitive language for the first time - it's simply something you've naturally been doing your whole life in most cases!

Your big picture, overall purpose for your life is joy.

Sounds so simple! And yet, true joy will call you to step up into your fullest potential - to no longer accept mediocrity or anything less than living a meaningful and fulfilling life.

Everything else is just a path we believe will get us there.

The money, success, accomplishment, recognition, validation, love, and freedom . . . they're all roads we believe will lead us to greater joy.

But if we're not careful, these can actually be detours when we focus on them. If, instead, we make joy our focus directly and immediately, we will expedite our momentum toward even greater joy a whole lot faster.

Make joy your focus, your filter for all decisions, and you will inevitably, and immediately, become in alignment with your highest and best path.

So the question then becomes: Which path will bring you the most joy? It's when you're in alignment with joy that you know you're on your soul's highest path!

Our inner compass is attuned to joy because joy truly is our highest calling and purpose.

Sound selfish?

Maybe. But you being in your highest state of joy is ultimately how you serve, inspire, and uplift others best.

I used to believe soul expansion was the purpose of being alive in human form. To experience things in human form that we cannot when we are in pure spirit form. This, however, led me down a detour of (unconsciously) also believing that the more I struggled and the more challenges and emotional turmoil I faced, the more evolved I was becoming. Because of this, I thought challenge and struggle were the way to live out my purpose. And though that may be the chosen life design of some old souls, I can see clearly now that I was creating unnecessary turmoil and strife in my life because I thought that was the whole point of being alive.

I did this by (most of it unknowingly):

- Making things harder than they needed to be;
- Torturing myself by over-analyzing every little decision;
- Working harder, and harder, and harder because that was the only way I deserved money or success;
- Believing the guilt-ridden, self-doubting inner critic bully inside my head;
- Never letting myself have too much money or too much success, as it would be disloyal to my family and friends;
- People-pleasing because it's my job to make sure everyone else is happy before I get to be happy myself.

Does any of this sound familiar, beauty?

While it is true that we can learn immensely from difficult times in our lives, that's not why we're here. We never said to ourselves before we were born, "Well, here I am in this blissful perfect place - get me out of here so I can go struggle somewhere else."

We chose to come to soul school, here on earth. A place of three-dimensional existence, contrast, light and dark, highs and lows, learning balance, having different feelings, and a range of emotions and experiences. This exciting adventure of remembering who we truly are at our core and having the courage to live in accordance with our highest truth.

Instead of believing that learning and expanding has to be hard, let it be easy. You've had fun learning new things before, right? Soul expansion can be fun, easy, and joyful, too.

Rather than taking these detours of hard work, struggle, uphill battles, emotional turmoil, financial difficulty, etc., etc. because of a belief that you are expanding your soul in this way... focus on joy, or rather, align with the inner compass of joy already within you, and you will be in alignment with your purpose.

Why?

Because your purpose of joy will call you to create a life that feels aligned with your soul - what feels good, what feels meaningful, and what feels fulfilling to you.

When we think we want more money, more time, more travel, nicer cars, nicer homes, nicer clothes, a sexier body - what we're really asking for is to feel better, to feel good, to feel joy.

And instead of looking for joy in the accumulation of external things - if we align our soul with feeling joy in our present moment, we will be filled up far more immensely than anything money could ever buy.

The fun part is, the more you fill your cup with joy from a higher place of presence, connectedness, inspired actions in your everyday life starting today, the more you will be in direct vibrational alignment which will then bring you even more joy, including the physical manifestations, too - such as money, travel, etc. You will have raised your vibration to be in alignment with those things, so now they can easily flow to you. Make sense?

So rather than focusing on the things that you think will bring you joy, focus on joy itself - living in joy, seeing joy, and basking in joy in your present, everyday life. By doing so, you will raise your vibration to the level of all things joy - where they can come to play with you in your reality.

What's important to note is by making joy your focus, aligning with it as your highest purpose, it does not mean everything is easy and you never grow, learn, or go through challenging times. I once thought if I chose to believe joy was my ultimate purpose, I would stop actually learning, growing, and expanding as a soul.

Does joy mean I just sit on the couch watching *The Bachelor* all day? Maybe sometimes! But usually, it's quite the opposite!

My joy calls me to become, and continue to journey toward, being the very highest and best version of myself, in all ways, at my own pace.

It wouldn't be joyful for me to just sit on the couch for the next sixty years and do nothing meaningful with my life.

My deepest sense of joy comes from serving and uplifting others. There's no greater feeling I've known than when I am speaking my truth, channeling from my soul, or when someone writes me with heartfelt gratitude over something I've shared, taught, or guided them with.

But it's not always easy for me to do this.

Moving in the direction of my highest joy calls me to become more vulnerable, to move well beyond my comfort zone over and over again. To go into the complete unknown financially, whether or not I will fail, and how other people will react to the "me" I am becoming. To put myself out there, to speak my truth even in the face of fear, to create things from my soul that maybe people won't even care about at all. To be a healthier version of myself. To eat better, to work out regularly even when I feel weak. To cry and lean on others when I need to, even though I'd always prided myself on being fiercely independent. To set loving boundaries between myself and people I very much love. To do things my ego will stop at nothing to convince me I can't.

Stepping into alignment with the ultimate purpose of joy has been one of the most challenging, and most deeply rewarding, journeys my soul has ever been on.

How each of us souls differ while we're here in human form is which path will ultimately bring us the most joy.

And this path does shift and evolve as you shift and evolve in different phases and stages of your life.

There may be a phase when motherhood brings you the most joy. There may be a phase when focusing on your physical fitness brings you the most joy. There may be a phase when starting your childhood dream business brings you the most joy. There may be a phase when working a job, receiving a steady paycheck, and just enjoying your life feels the most joyful for you. And there may be a phase of life when finding balance in each area of your life is your most joyful focus.

What is it for you, dear soul? What brings you your deepest sense of joy, at this stage of your life?

What could bring you an even deeper, fuller sense of joy?

If you're completely lost when it comes to these questions right now, don't worry. We'll dig deep together and help you gain clarity in the coming chapters.

I can't speak for you or for every human on the planet, of course. But something inside tells me that we all desire to feel as though our life matters. That we made a difference, someway, somehow, by being here - usually through our positive impact in the lives of others.

By being the best mother we could, by being the best daughter we could, a caring sister, a nurturing friend, a loving wife - maybe even in our professional life by being a rockstar receptionist, a compassionate nurse, a genuine salesperson, a positive boss, a friendly coffee barista, an inspiring CEO, an encouraging peer.

Perhaps we even feel called to leverage our life experience - the things we have faced, the challenges we have overcome - and create a business that allows us to turn around and help others currently going through the same thing. Through social media, blogging, vlogging, programs, courses, coaching, mentoring, consulting…

What's running through your mind right now, my friend? Better yet, what's coming up through your soul?

Before we move deeper into uncovering your own purpose, take a moment now to close your eyes, relax your breathing, and ask yourself, "What excites me now?"

Without any filter, judgement, or rejection, be curious about the very first instinctual thing(s) that come up for you. Make a note of them if you like, as we carry on with discovering your purpose, your ultimate path to joy.

Our purpose in life isn't to arrive at a destination where we find inspiration, Just as the purpose of dancing isn't to end up at a particular spot on the floor. The purpose of dancing and of life is to enjoy every moment and every step, regardless of where we are when the music ends.
~ Dr. Wayne Dyer

CHAPTER 13

How To Uncover Your Personal Path To Purpose

"The heart of human excellence often begins to beat when you deliver a pursuit that absorbs you, frees you, challenges you, or gives you a sense of meaning, joy, or passion."
~ Terry Orlick

I've been fortunate enough to work with countless women on finding their purpose. And though we now know that our ultimate purpose is to live a life dedicated to joy, we do each have our own unique path that will lead us to greater and greater joy.

For example, when I was eighteen-years-old working as a hostess at a family restaurant, all I wanted was to be a server. I wanted to have fun conversations with people enjoying a night out, earn tips, and go spend them on having fun with my friends.

When I became a server, I did really enjoy making tips, but I also got the clarity that serving didn't feel as joyful for me as I had thought it would. I now felt like a stable job with stable shifts, steady income, and evenings and weekends off would be incredible!

So I got a job as a finance assistant and eventually become a mortgage broker. At first, I was thrilled! Every weekend off! Knowing my hours weeks and months in advance so I could make plans, knowing what my income would be - it was fantastic! For a while . . .

Until I realized I didn't love trading forty hours a week of my life for something I had zero passion for. Instead, I realized that I wanted to spend my forty-hour work week doing something I actually *loved*.

Enter photography. The childhood dream that (almost) got away. I *loved* creating this dream, even though it took me getting over massive amounts of fear in order to do so. Remember, moving in the direction of our joy calls us to move beyond what's comfortable!

I couldn't believe I was actually getting paid to do something I loved so much I'd do it for free!

And then BOOM - a realization that I'd rather be shouting the message of limitless possibility from the rooftops for other people to experience, too, rather than to keep living it (just) for myself.

And here we are. I feel more ignited, aligned, and purposeful than ever before with the work I do now. But I had to follow the dots, the breadcrumbs of joy, in order to get here.

Imagine if instead, at eighteen-years-old, I just waited around wondering what my "big" thing was, my "big" purpose. I would have stayed stuck forever at a job I didn't love.

I needed to move forward with one joy breadcrumb at a time.

Now it's your turn.

Make a list of everything you *love*, appreciate, and are grateful for in your life right now. Keep going until you completely run out of things to be thankful for. A beating heart, at least one functioning lung, food in the fridge, one really great friend, fresh air, hot showers, etc. Name it, all of it. And when you think you're done, keep going.

The point of this list is to help you see just how awesome your life already is. The fact that you're even alive is a gift - one that some pretty great people no longer have. And while I'm not encouraging you to become complacent, I do want you to shift your energy by loving your life right now - so you will become a vibrational match for a life you actually increasingly love more and more and more.

When that list has been entirely exhausted, make a list of desires. What would you like to feel more of in your life? What would you like to get better at? What would you like to learn more about or learn how to do? What do you wish you had more of? What do you wish was different?

When you look at people you're envious of - friends, people on social media - what is it that you think they have, that you want?

This list will start giving you clues, just like the clues I had about desiring to earn tips, then desiring to have weekends off, then desiring to do something I was more passionate about, then desiring to do something that felt more fulfilling and meaningful to me.

I feel like I can hear you wondering, *What is it that would make me feel more fulfilled?*

And that is an excellent question to ask your inner guide.

Grab a journal and pen and have a conversation with yourself, without *any* filter between your heart and your pen (do NOT let your head get in the way). No judgement, no thinking, no delay - just ask the question, and write the *first* thing that comes through you.

What would excite me now?

If I could do ANYTHING - without any worry at all about fear, money, time, etc. - how would I spend my time?

Where would I be?

Who would I be with?

What would I be doing?

If I were capable of *anything* - without any self-judgement or limitation - what do I wish I could do?

Describe the most unapologetic, ultimate, highest version of you. What does she look like? How does she think? What does she wear? How does she feel each day? How does she spend her time? What does she do for a living?

And what is she doing differently than you?

We can actually go really deep with this work and uncover your specific purpose path. Have a peek at the Purpose Clarity free resource I made for you at *jenniferjayde.com/theawakeningbook*

For now the best thing you can do (trust me on this), is relieve yourself of searching for a big answer and instead follow the dots of joy - day by day.

Fresh air, a book, a nap, a podcast. A walk in nature, meditation. Maybe a trip for a day, a weekend, a week.

Play around with learning more about the things that interest you. Reach out and connect with people you feel are working within the vicinity of something you'd like to do. Ask them how they got started.

I've found that when I'm looking really hard for something, I never find it. So I let it go, I trust the journey, and I just focus on enjoying my life as much as I can. When I relax into this space, the answers always reveal themselves, in exact divine timing.

Trust! :)

If you can tune into your purpose
and really align with it,
Setting goals so that your vision is
an expression of that purpose,
Then life flows much more easily.
– Jack Canfield

The answers always reveal themselves, in exact divine timing.

~ Jennifer Jayde

The Awakening

CHAPTER 14

Getting Aligned with Your Highest Path

*"The things that bring you the greatest joy are
in alignment with your purpose."*
~ Jack Canfield

Even though our ultimate, overall purpose is joy - both experiencing it in the present moment and moving toward an even greater sense of joy with our daily actions and decisions - one of the things I can see so clearly now in hindsight is that life has a way of preparing us to step into our highest, most joyful paths all along.

For example, the work I do now - helping people to truly align with their highest selves, uncover their (unique) highest purpose, and live their best lives - brings me my greatest sense of joy (aka my purpose), but this work was only made possible through a lifelong series of events that led me here. The most pivotal being the not-so-great ones.

My drive and ambition was born from fearing the lack and scarcity I witnessed in my household as a child.

My desire to quit my nine-to-five and pursue my childhood dream of destination wedding photography only got kicked into action after witnessing a family member slowly succumb to disease at age forty-two.

My desire to leave a thriving photography business and serve as many people as possible in the creation of their own dreams was brought to life because I thought (initially) that I had a duty to save everyone from the misery that I once felt in my nine-to-five.

I can only really connect and understand these dots in hindsight - I didn't realize it when I was in the moment, living them. And these are just a few very basic ones to share as an example.

Often when working with my clients, I find that when we take a deeper look into their past, we find clues as to what future they would desire to create most.

This doesn't necessarily mean that you have to have endured hardships in order to have a purpose. Remember, your ultimate purpose is joy. Joy in your present moment, and even greater joy as you move along. This has nothing to do with whether or not you've endured hardships in your past.

What I do find is that contribution is a major factor to joy and feelings of purpose and meaning.

And our contributions often stem from things that have affected us in some way. This experience triggered our desire to help or be of service in any way possible. To learn more about it,and then to share our knowledge, experience, and wisdom with others.

If you were to scan through your past right now, what experiences, circumstances, or events stand out to you as playing a major role in who you've become today?

If it helps, think about your upbringing. What kind of parents did you have? In what ways did your upbringing shape the person you are now?

What about your childhood? Did you have to move a lot? Did you have any experiences that affected who you've become?

What is your favorite experience of your life? Why? How has that changed and developed you?

All of these things are clues as to what you could contribute to others that would feel absolutely meaningful and powerful for you. And because of this, bring you immense joy.

Which, as you know, is your purpose.

After you've had an opportunity to explore your past for clues, we can also scan your present for more.

If you were to make a list of all things that you feel intrigued to learn more about right now, what would they include? No filter or self-judgement allowed . . .

Would you want to take a hip-hop dance class? Learn calligraphy? Take Italian language classes? Learn to paint?

Learn photography? Write a book? Take up sailing?

Make a list of anything and everything you're intrigued by right now, and keep going until you run out.

Let's think about what's already been drawing you in lately. Who have you been following on social media? Why? What do they speak, share, or teach about? What are they an example of? What makes you keep going back to check their profiles?

What books have you been reading? What podcasts or audiobooks have you been listening to? What have you been watching on Youtube or searching on Google?

What is your favorite topic to talk about with friends or people you meet with this common interest?

What is the thing you could talk about for hours and lose track of time?

What courses or workshops have you been taking or been tempted to take?

Make a list of all the things you'd love to be, know, do, and have, right now - if you could!

And when you're done that list, move on to our last section . . .

Anytime I'm feeling stuck or stagnant in my life, I ask myself one question. As long as I'm open to anything, I get instant feedback that helps guide me forward.

I ask, "What excites me now?"

I'll close my eyes and daydream. Sometimes I'll hear "my own thoughts" provide words or phrases about things I'd love to be doing now or in the future. Sometimes I'll get visions of where I am, what I'm doing, and with whom. I'll see what I look like, how I dress, where I live. I let my mind freely and limitlessly take me on a journey of infinite possibility.

And a few minutes later, I journal this all down to grasp what just came through.

By doing this, you'll get clues about your "big picture" vision of where your soul longs to be. And though you may not understand or even see the straight-up HOW to make this happen, at least now you have something to plug into your inner GPS. Then trust that the Universe will help guide you along your path of least resistance to getting there.

For example, let's say you see yourself being able work from home to live and work from anywhere in the world. There's no office you have to report to each day.

You see yourself living in a mansion somewhere warm, on a cliff overlooking the beach, doing yoga each morning from your ocean view balcony.

You're not quite sure what specifically you're doing for income each day, but you know that it feels good, spacious, and meaningful to you. It completely lights you up without draining or overwhelming you. And hey, you only work a few hours a day, a few days per week!

These are all clues to the path with which you can align your heart, soul, and next steps, even when you don't know what those are right now.

To help you even further with this, I've created a guided meditation called *Find Your Purpose Meditation + Workbook*. You can access this at: jenniferjayde.com/theawakeningbook

The way forward does not come from figuring out how to get to where you want to go, but from trusting the inner guidance (sparks of joy) along the way - and taking the inspired action forward, even when your head (inner critic) can't make sense of it and is trying everything it can to stop you.

Remember, your ultimate purpose is joy. Joy in your present moment, and even greater joy as you move along.
~ Jennifer Jayde

*If you find yourself eating or
spending in excess, remember this:
If you want to feel full, do
something that fulfills you.
If you want to feel rich – serve.
– Jennifer Jayde*

5

Aligning with Your Soul

CHAPTER 15

Six Steps To A Higher Level Of Soul Alignment

"Just as your car runs more smoothly and requires less energy to go faster and farther when the wheels are in perfect alignment, you perform better when your thoughts, feelings, emotions, goals, and values are in balance."
~ Brian Tracy

I used to be so afraid to declare what it was I really wanted in my life. At times, I had set goals and intentions, and they never came to fruition. I was left disappointed, sad, and beating myself up, so I stopped dreaming so big. I stopped setting goals. I stopped asking for things that I felt were outside of my reach because I wanted to save myself from the disappointment.

But you don't get what you don't ask for. I think of the Universe kinda like Santa Clause. Imagine if you went and sat on

Santa's knee, and he asked you what you wanted, and you just said, "I don't know. I don't want anything. I don't need anything," or "I don't know, Santa, you pick. I won't say anything. I'll let you decide."

Maybe you remember Christmas or birthdays when you didn't ask for what you wanted, and you ended up with that pair of socks or that doll that you never really cared about. It kind of works that way with the Universe, too. We need to find a way to ask for what it is we truly want - the big picture, the big dream, the big desire - but to detach our self-worth from the result, from whether or not we get it in the way and in the timing that our ego self is trying to control and dictate.

I thought the best thing would be to just stop setting any goals and having any clear desires. This just lead to life happening to me, instead of me being the creator of my life.

What I've come to realize is that you can absolutely ask the Universe for what you want, but you must then trust in what you receive. From that vantage point, you can then ask for what you want next or where you want to go from there. This creates the effect of forward momentum in a direction you actually want to pursue. *One foot in front of the other, big life transformations actually happen in small steps over time.* You get to design and create a life that you love in collaboration with the Universe.

There are six steps, six things to remember if you would like to be on the most streamlined, fastest route to be, do, and have anything you desire - because you truly are limitless. You've just got to be willing to ask for what you want.

#1 - Unapologetic Ownership

Unapologetically declare what you desire. Think big, dream big. Don't be afraid to put it out there, to admit to yourself what it is you truly want. Declare it. Write it in your journal in the back of this book. What is it that you really want? Where do you want to live? What view do you want to have when you look out your window?

How do you want to dress? How often do you want to get your hair done? How often do you want to have a massage or a spa day? How often do you want to be able to treat your friends to a girls' trip or a concert? What kind of vehicle do you wish you could drive? What kind of home do you want to live in? How much often would you like to travel? How would you like to be traveling? First Class, business class, private jet, limo, luxury RV? The sky's not the limit - it's just the beginning. You are an infinite, limitless being. Ask unapologetically for what you desire. Declare what you desire. Describe it with all five senses. Be vivid in your explanation. Feel what it feels like for these things to become your reality, and make a list of those feelings.

What are the deep desired feelings that this list of desires evokes? Are they freedom, passion, fulfillment, excitement, adventure, spontaneity, inner peace, happiness, joy, bliss? Write it all down...

#2 - Feel The Fear And Do It Anyway

Remember what we learned in Part Two: Freedom from Fear. We learned about the ego. We learned about fears. We learned about how the survival instinct in our brain wants to keep us small, wants to keep us dim, wants to keep us within the known and the familiar to keep us alive and surviving.

So when we begin to unapologetically declare what we desire, it may trigger this ego part to start speaking up, to start chiming in. To start instilling fear into us. It's now time for you to put into practice what you've been learning throughout this book. Become the observer of your thoughts and your fears, but do not live in them. Observe that they're there, but don't allow them to get in your way. Do not allow them to stop you. They're not real, and you know that now.

I'll never forget how much fear, self-doubt, and sleepless nights I faced, with my ego, my inner critic screaming at me not to leave my nine-to-five job. Screaming that I should just be more grateful and do what would make my parents proud, fit in with society, and make sure that I had money coming in. I thought I was going crazy because I had one loud inner voice telling me not to do something and then another one whispering to go ahead and see what was possible if I truly followed my heart.

What's really great is the more you feel the fear and do it anyway, the easier it becomes the next time, and the next time, and the next time.

So when you're being bombarded with self-doubt, with your inner critic, with fears, ego, and worry, take a step back and lean back into the truth of who you really are. Observe these thoughts and these worries as what they truly are - illusions created by ego that no longer have the dictatorship over your life. So many people have asked me when the fearful thoughts will go away so they can finally move forward with what they want. The truth is, those fearful thoughts never go away. So if we wait until we feel ready, until we feel good about doing something new in our lives and really going after what we want, *we will be waiting for the rest of our lives*. The moment often never comes when we feel one hundred percent confident in moving into something new. There will always be that fear, that inner critic, that ego coming in to try and convince us to stay where it's safe, where the known and familiar reside.

#3 - Vibrate What You Wish For

Remember (*always* remember) - what you focus on expands. Remember your deep desired feelings. Do whatever you need to do to remind yourself of these feelings several times a day, every day. So if you desire to feel freedom, if you desire to feel abundance, if you desire to feel passion, if you desire to feel adventure, focus on these feelings in your everyday life and pay attention to where you're already experiencing them, moment by moment, in the pockets of your day. When you give these feelings your focus, when you really feel the appreciation for these feelings when they're happening, you are pouring gas on the fire, creating more and more and more of the feelings you want. If you really do want to take the fastest route to anything you want to be, do, or have - focus on what feels good. Focus on what feels in alignment with your deep desired feelings, and when it excites you to do something that you've never done before, trust that inner guidance, and go beyond your current comfort zone.

Remember that in between where you are now and that desire that you're being drawn toward, there are going to be those fears from the ego coming up. Remember that you're the observer of these thoughts and that you don't have to believe them anymore, and keep bringing your attention back to what's good. What is in alignment with how you desire to feel?

The Universe is in a constant state of "your wish is my command," and it doesn't speak English - it only understands vibration. So if you are saying, "I want more money," but your vibration is more like, "I don't have enough" - the Universe can only understand the latter and respond within your reality with more lack.

How do we change this then? Manage your focus. Instead of focusing on what's lacking, focus on where you are abundant. You are rich with air to breathe, water to drink, food to eat, grass to walk on, clothing, shoes, dishes, cups, a warm place to sleep, a sun that shines nonstop . . .

Some people ask me if they need to be in control of their thoughts 24/7, and the answer is absolutely not. That would be way too exhausting. Go about your life and do your best to feel good, to see the bright side, to see the blessing even throughout the burdens. When you're feeling good, when you're feeling joy, when you're feeling your deep desired feelings, you don't need to concern yourself with your thoughts. The only time you need to reassess what you're thinking about is when you're starting to dip below feeling good. That's the only time you need to check in to see where your thoughts have gone. Because when this happens, your mind has drifted off into autopilot, and when our mind goes on autopilot, it tends to drift toward the negative, the burdens, the unhappy thoughts. So you don't have to be in control of your thoughts 24/7, but you should tune in when you are feeling less than happy. That's the time to refocus your thoughts, be conscious of what you're focusing on, and ask yourself if it is serving you or not.

#4 - When The Student Is Ready, The Teacher Appears

Now it's time to welcome your teachers in all their many guises. Some of them will literally be teachers. Some of them will be coaches. Some of them will be mentors. Some will be children, some will be strangers, some will be your family and the ways in which they trigger you and / or inspire you.

But if and when you come across somebody who is willing to teach you or guide you toward something that excites you and your intuition is nudging you to work with them - do it. They have been brought along on your path for a reason. If you have to move heaven and earth to make it happen, do it. If it terrifies you to make the investment, to spend money you don't actu- ally have yet - do it. Honestly, I know how this feels, but I also know that when I continue to do things just in the way I know how, nothing changes. When I wanted my financial situation to change, I needed someone outside of my own mind to help me make those changes that I clearly wasn't making for myself, and I needed to invest in their time and energy in order to receive the benefits of working with them. Money is ultimately an ener- gy exchange. That's why it's called currency.

#5 - Happiness Isn't The Destination, It Is the Path Of Least Resistance (to More Happiness!)

Remember to make your life's priority your daily priority.

So often in my life, I have focused on one particular area because I thought gaining success in that area would make me happier. There were times when I focused so much on growing my finance business. When I was in my nine-to-five, I worked so hard to make more money because I thought once I made just a little bit more, I would be happier. I was miserable in my job, but I thought making more money in that job would make me happier.

I was wrong, so I created my dream photography business

and I worked really, really, really, really hard because I thought the more money I made in my photography business, the happier I would be. This led to burnout. This lead to exhaustion. This led to me becoming imbalanced in other areas of my life. I didn't see my husband as much. I didn't see my friends very often. My health started to fall by the wayside.

So then I became really focused on being healthy and fit, and I dedicated a lot of attention, focus, time, and energy into it.

I hired more mentors, more teachers. I was working out once or twice a day, almost every day. Then my business started falling by the wayside because I thought health and fitness would make me happier. When I looked a certain way, when I released these last five or ten pounds, then I would be happy.

What I've learned is thinking that something outside of me is going to make me happier actually pulls me out of balance in all other areas of my life. Instead, when I make joy my priority, everything else falls into place - in a joyful way.

So when I am joyful and grateful for my body the way it is, and I really appreciate all that it does for me - my heart beating for me and my lungs breathing for me and my organs filtering everything and my skin healing my cuts - I also want to fuel it in a loving way. I want to move it in a loving way. So not only can I love my body the way that it is, but that love for my body inspires me to treat it in a loving way with great nutrition and proper, fun exercise, not punishing exercise.

When I love my business the way that it is, even if it is not my biggest grand vision for my life and my business in this moment, I no longer want to hold my breath for days, months, years for this big vision to arrive, for a big grand day that may never come. All that would mean is that I spent my entire life holding my breath, waiting for a certain circumstance before I could be happy. Instead, I could love my business, my income, my job right now as it is, even if it's not my grand vision, while I'm working toward what excites me now. And by doing that, not only am I happy in the moment, but I also am creating action in alignment with joy. I'm creating more income in alignment with joy. I'm growing my business in alignment with joy.

When we put a circumstance or an outcome ahead of our happiness, it's like we're holding our breath and we're pinching ourselves off from being happy until that circumstance or outcome comes to play. This means we're constantly telling ourselves that we can't be happy until this happens, until that happens. And what are we saying to the Universe? That we're not happy. So what are we holding in our vibration? That we're not happy. And what does the Universe do? Respond to our vibration with more things to be unhappy about.

Prioritizing joy will help all other things fall into place in such a greater, more joyful, pleasurable way, and enjoyable way.

Sometimes I think about things from a hindsight perspective, even if I haven't lived them yet. I'll think about a decision or something as if I were viewing it from my deathbed. This is how I can really do a gut check to see whether my priorities in my daily life are aligning with my overall life's priorities. And if you think about it, what is your overall life's priority? Is it to live life to the fullest? Is it to live a life without regrets? Is it to be adventurous? To explore, to see all that you can become, to see all the lives that you can impact, to have as much fun as you possibly can and laugh as many times as you possibly can and hug your family and create as many memories with them as you possibly can? Are these the things that you're going to be grateful for on your deathbed?

Well then, come back to your daily life and ask yourself, "Are those the things I'm making my priority, or am I putting everything else first?"

"Sorry, dear, I can't talk now, I have to get to these emails."

"Oh sorry, kids, um, we can't do that this weekend. I have to go do this work thing."

"I can't get to the gym because I have to make money. So I've got to, you know, attend to all of these clients or potential clients first."

So often, I catch myself and my clients putting the wrong things first because we've all put this outcome between ourselves and our happiness. And then we're in this race to get to this outcome so that we can finally be happy. But that's backwards. Find the things that you can be happy for and make your lifetime priority your daily priority. Make sure these priorities are in alignment with each other.

#6 - Small Steps Over Time Lead To Incredible Results

If you want to take the fastest route to be, do, and have anything you desire, take your eyes off the top of the mountain - that big dream, that big vision, that big desire, that big hope, that big goal - and bring your focus back down to your own two feet. Forget about what steps two through twelve are, and just focus on that one tiny baby step forward that you could take today.

Just be playful with it. Be curious and don't let your mind drift off into, "Oh, but what about step three and step four and?

How am I going to get to step six? And what if it doesn't work at step seven? And how am I going to make money and how's this gonna work? And what if this? And what if that?"

The further you think into the future, the deeper you sink into overwhelm. Your mind, your ego, your inner critic will take you to terrible, terrifying places if you let it. So come back to the present. Look at your own two feet. Not at what Susie over here is doing and at what Lisa over there is doing and how they did it, and what's worked for them. Really stay focused on you, your path, your journey, what excites you now in this moment, and just slide your foot forward. One baby step first. Your baby steps will turn into regular strides. Your regular strides will turn into jogging. Your jogging will turn into running. Your running will turn into sprinting, and your sprinting will turn into flying. But it starts with baby steps. You've really got to come back to the present and focus on that baby step because as long as you are staring at the top of the mountain and telling yourself you don't know how to fly, you won't know how to get to the top of that mountain. You will stay stuck at the base. Baby steps - because taking small steps over time will take you a heck of a lot further than taking zero steps because you're stuck in overwhelm.

Massive transformations happen one small step at a time.

Deep within, you know that the
only thing that is truly important
is being in alignment with spirit.
~ Dr. Wayne Dyer

CHAPTER 16

Weeding The Roots That Are Tying You Down

"You must find a place inside yourself where nothing is impossible."
~ Deepak Chopra

When I first started going through my life coach certification, one of the things we were taught is that we learn fifty percent of everything we know between birth and eight-years-old. It's within these ages that we had no filter, no screen for our subconscious mind, so we absorbed everything our childhood brain perceived as truth. Regardless of whether we had the most perfect parents or if we had deadbeat parents or somewhere in the middle, what it boils down to is how we viewed them and perceived their actions as children. That sunk down into our subconscious mind as truth.

Maybe we took on the belief that money doesn't grow on trees and that you have to work really, really, really, hard in order to earn a decent living. Maybe we saw rich people as greedy and selfish. Maybe we saw poor people as lazy. Maybe we didn't want to surpass the level of success our parents had reached so as not to embarrass them or leave them behind in any way. Whatever it is, these subconscious burdens, these subconscious weeds and roots will stay there, buried and hidden deep in our subconscious mind (from which we operate eight or ninety percent every single day) - unless we do something to change it.

How do you know if you have a subconscious root that needs to be pulled, that needs to be plucked, that needs to be removed? By reflecting back on your life, observing how it is at present, and becoming aware of the patterns you have that are not serving you. Maybe you continually take one step forward and two steps back in your finances. Maybe you're having a hard time building a deep relationship with a partner. Maybe you're an entrepreneur, and your business success has plateaued. There are so many different patterns and outcomes with which we can limit ourselves without really understanding why.

I'm going to share with you four main roots that I've observed in myself and in hundreds of my clients over the last few years. These roots have really been holding us back from stepping into full alignment with our soul's potential. See if you recognize yourself in any of these subconscious roots.

#1 - The Burden Root

The burden root shows up in doing anything so as not to be a burden to others. You may have an underlying belief from childhood that you are an annoyance or in the way, or that it's rude to ask for what you want. More symptoms include: people-pleasing, saying yes when you really mean no, putting everyone else first and putting your needs and desires last, not asking for help or for your needs to be met by anyone else.

Does any of this sound familiar at all?

What about feeling constantly drained and exhausted from taking the world on your own shoulders so as not to burden anyone else with your problems? You may actually prefer to be away from other people; perhaps you don't feel comfortable being yourself but rather find yourself acting as an acceptable version of yourself when around others - being more like a chameleon than your true self...

#2 - The Dimming Root

The belief behind the dimming root is that it's a crime for you to shine and fully own your magnificence because it might make others feel badly about themselves. This could mean your siblings, your parents, your co-workers, your friends, your family, even strangers. Symptoms of the dimming root could look like deflecting compliments and acknowledgements from others and / or over analyzing yourself constantly. Second-guessing yourself and staying stuck in self-torment and indecision as an unconscious method of self-sabotage. Finding ways to stay small, not being able to see opportunity, even deflecting opportunity. Shying away from opportunity for falsely rationalized reasons, and passing along the credit to someone or something else.

#3 - The Unsafe / Unsupported Root

The hidden self-limiting belief behind this root is that it's unsafe to rely on anything or anyone outside of yourself. Symptoms of this could be subconscious or conscious thoughts like, "I am an independent woman and it is weak to rely or lean on others," or "If you want something done right, you must do it yourself," or "No one can support me better than I can." Needing to control outcomes, circumstances, or how things happen and when. Being afraid of or unclear on surrender, worried about money, or feeling like it's never enough, you always need more. Not trusting others' advice or help or second-guessing their intentions. Running around making sure everyone else feels supported in the ways that you never did.

#4 - The External Validation Root

The subconscious tape playing for somebody with the external validation root is that they were never validated / acknowledged as a child for the things that were meaningful to them, so maybe they felt like their parents didn't care or didn't take any notice. They felt like they were never validated, congratulated, acknowledged, and so now they seek that acknowledgement elsewhere.

For example, we may place excessive value on social media likes and comments, achievement in any form, credentials, income, recognition, awards. We could also seek validation from the size of our business growth, the number of clients we have, the number of testimonials we receive. How many people thank us for helping them and tell us that we're so good at what we do. Maybe the validation comes from surrounding ourselves with material things and status symbols. Another symptom is seeking external validation from men, from partners, from relationships, from feeling loved by others. We can place this need for external validation on our physical appearance, our weight or body shape, our clothing size, our fitness level. We may seek words of affirmation and validation from others and be in an inner state of turmoil when we do not receive validation in the way we had hoped.

While these tend to be the four main roots, there are a couple more to consider. One is the self-worth root. One variation of this root says, "If I never play a hundred percent full out, I can always rationalize why I failed." We can attach our self-worth to almost anything. We can attach it to an outcome. We can attach it to a goal or an intention, and if our self-worth is attached to an outcome, we'll find that we are constantly on an emotional rollercoaster ride depending on the results of these outcomes. This emotional rollercoaster ride can be quite draining and is not necessary.

Another root to consider is the disloyalty root, which says, "If I am successful or more prosperous than my friends and family, I'm being disloyal and leaving them behind."

So tell me, my friend, do you resonate with any of these roots?

Even though they may not be something that you consciously believe to be true anymore, is there a part of you that recognizes yourself and your life?

If so, there's a very good chance that some of these roots were planted even before you have memory of creating them, somewhere between the ages of zero and eight-years-old. The good news is that you can absolutely uproot these beliefs now. They no longer have to act as the anchors holding you back in your life. Abraham Hicks says, *"A belief is simply a thought we've had playing on repeat."* A belief is simply a thought we've had playing on repeat, so if you would like to change your beliefs (and therefore your vibration and your reality), it's time to change the thoughts you're listening to on repeat. How do we do this? Repetition is one of the most powerful ways to reprogram the subconscious mind.

I've put this to the test for myself and have been pretty blown away with the results. They were small and slow at first, but the longer I stayed committed, the bigger and faster my momentum became.

I created a recording using a paragraph of mantras and affirmations that I really knew I needed to reprogram in my own mind and in my own vibration. I took this paragraph and I repeated it eight times in a row into the voice recorder of my phone. Every night before bed, I put my phone into airplane mode and then power it off so that in the morning when I turn it back on, I have no notifications beeping or buzzing or distracting me. I plug in my ear buds while I'm still half asleep, in between snooze buttons on my alarm clock, and I listen to this recording every morning.

If you put this into practice for at least thirty days, ***if you will commit*** to making this a practice for thirty days, you will see your outer reality shift and align with what you've placed in this recording. Be open to noticing the shifts. Acknowledge the shifts. Give silent gratitude every time you notice the shifts, because what you focus on expands. (And if you could use some help with this, I've created a free guideline for you called *The New Reality Morning Practice* over at jenniferjayde.com/theawakening

Recall, the Universe is in a constant state of "your wish is my command," and it's speaking vibration. *This is how you change your vibration into one that serves you and not one that limits you.* You can also release yourself from these roots through the cord cutting exercises described earlier in this book, visualizations, and making new choices day by day, opportunity by opportunity, moment by moment.

So the next time you're considering dimming yourself when writing a social media post or when speaking to your spouse or your parents, shift in that moment and choose differently. You can start small and work your way up to bigger and bigger shifts over time, but it's in those small choices, moment by moment, day by day, that you will notice that gravity of the changes you're making. Remember that you are an infinite being created from and of the Universe. You are capable of anything and are absolutely limitless. Continue your morning ritual, practice grounding yourself into Mother Earth's energy and connecting yourself to Source. Remember your infiniteness. Your limitlessness. You were born worthy, born loved unconditionally, and it's time for you to lift your chin up, stick your chest out, and own your greatness. Any other attachment does not serve you - and you can let it go today.

Just as a baby doesn't have to earn your love, you, too, were born into unconditional love. Love is not earned through dimming or people-pleasing or anything else. Own it, and walk forward from here being whoever you want to be, knowing that you will continue to be loved unconditionally.

Remember your infiniteness.
Your limitlessness.
You were born worthy,
born loved unconditionally,
and it's time for you to lift
your chin up, stick your chest out,
and own your greatness.
~ Jennifer Jayde

Wear gratitude like a cloak and it will feed every corner of your life.
~ Rumi

CHAPTER 17

Navigating Your Emotional Guidance System

"When you are grateful, fear disappears and abudance appears."
~ Tony Robbins

Not too long ago, I was chatting on the phone with my colleague and good friend, Ariel Frey, and I was surprised when she said to me, "I don't care about other people's feelings." That took me aback a bit, as someone who has made a habit of taking on and trying to solve other people's feelings and problems, for family and friends, colleagues and clients, financially, emotionally, physically, and spiritually. This comment came right out of left field, smacked me across the face, and left me with my jaw on the ground. Needless to say, I was intrigued.

Ariel went on to explain that it wasn't so much that she

didn't care about other people's feelings, but more that she was no longer taking responsibility for other people's feelings. Something in my soul said, *Pay attention to this.* So I kept listening. Ariel told me that when we take ownership and responsibility for our own feelings, we are no longer victims of other people's thoughts, opinions, or comments. Additionally, we also set ourselves free to speak our truth and be who we really are. We can be one hundred percent authentic because we are no longer attached to how that may make other people feel. We spend so much of our life dimming down and shying away from speaking our truth and being our full selves out of fear of how it may be received or perceived by other people and how it may make them feel, eventually we are nothing but an empty shell of our true selves. But when we learn to take responsibility for our own feelings, we are all free to be who we really are. And if something someone else says triggers us, rather than playing the blame game, we can use that to explore what really is asking to be brought up into the light to be healed, forgiven, and released.

I can't say that I no longer care about other people's feelings, but I'm so grateful for this lesson that I am not responsible for everybody else's feelings.

Where in your life have you been taking responsibility for the feelings of the people around you? Have you done yourself a disservice by being untrue to who you are, what you believe, and what you really wanted to say or do? Maybe you've been financially supporting someone when you don't actually have the extra money to do so. Maybe you've been giving your time when in reality, you do need that time for yourself, for your own needs and your own desires.

I am not saying to never help another person or to never be there for someone else, but I am saying to put your needs first, take responsibility for yourself, for your own feelings and your needs, and allow others the space and respect to do the same for themselves. You're not here to save everyone else. You're not here to play God in anyone else's life. Everyone is their own ultimate creator of their reality and you are the ultimate creator of your reality. Nobody else's.

So take that thousand-pound weight off your chest that you've been carrying, trying to fix, help, and save everyone else. It's not your job. It's not your responsibility. Your job, your responsibility is your own happiness.

When you do get triggered by another person's words or actions, it is an amazing gift in disguise. It is showing a part of you that is ready to be healed. It is not what the person or did that is actually what's upsetting you. Instead, the trigger is reminding you of something left unhealed in your soul. Many times it's something from your childhood that has not been healed. It's like a sliver coming up to the surface that's now ready to poke through and be released.

When you are triggered, it's absolutely natural and human to have an emotional reaction. You may feel sad, you may feel hurt, you may feel angry, you may feel frustrated - that is absolutely okay. There was a time when I made the mistake of thinking it wasn't okay to have negative emotions. I thought that I had to think and act positively all the time, or I would manifest something bad into my life and into my reality. So I never gave myself any time or space to be sad or angry.

Like we discussed in Chapter 9, you can't ignore emotional energy away. You can store some sadness in your cup, but the more you're storing and suppressing your emotions, the more that cup starts to fill up. Eventually the cup overflows.

One thing to pay attention to is if you're ever feeling an emotion, but you don't understand its source.. I remember working with my first life coach, the late James Butler. He asked me a question during one of our sessions that left me feeling astonished, "Jen, do you sometimes feel sad for no reason?" Talk about being in tune with your client because I was absolutely feeling random bouts of sadness and feeling them quite often during those times just before I started working with James. He asked, "Do you want to know how I knew that?" And I said yes, because I'm starting to get a little creeped out by how he would even know this. And he said, "Jen, you are not comfortable expressing anger, and if you don't allow yourself to express anger, then that emotion is going to spill over into the next cup, which is sadness, and pour out of you in that way. So you might find yourself feeling sad and not even understanding what made you sad in the first place."

The opposite may be true as well. Maybe it's easier for you to express anger than it is sadness. And so you find yourself being easily triggered, easily angered, and not really understanding why.

The good news however, is there are so many ways you can express this energy and it doesn't have to be right there in the moment when you're experiencing it - that you don't have to blow up at someone in grocery store, right? You can go home, figure out, release this emotional energy in whatever way feels good for you and then when you're ready and when you've released that cup of emotional energy, get curious as to why that actually really triggered you. What's the real root reason that you were triggered? Often you'll find if you dig deep enough, it had nothing to do with that particular incident.

Not too long ago, it was my birthday. At that time, there was somebody in my life for whom I had (in my mind, at least) bent over backwards for time and time again. I was being that person who was giving extra money that I didn't have to give. Who was giving extra time that I didn't have to give. Who was saying yes when I really meant no. Who was doing things out of alignment with myself and my goals and my dreams and my desires because I felt like I had to be there for this person. I thought I had to come to this person's rescue. I'm not just talking about once or twice - I'm talking about a period of several years, over and over and over again. I knew that this person had bought other people birthday cards and even birthday presents. But when my birthday rolled around, I didn't even get a card. This really stung. It really hurt, honestly - even if they didn't have the money, a handmade card or just anything would have felt so nice to receive. At the time, I thought I needed this validation, and I thought that I had earned it and that I deserved it from this person. Some kind of acknowledgement, even with no monetary value, after everything I had done for them.

Now this really triggered me. But I know by now that when I'm triggered, there's something deeper going on. Surely I couldn't be this upset over a birthday card, because I was *really* upset. I couldn't even sleep that night. I was tossing and turning in the middle of the night, and I came upon this Youtube video of a TedX talk by Mandy Saligari called *Feelings: Handle them before they handle you*.[4] It changed everything for me. It was that "ah-ha" moment that I needed right then.

What I learned from this video is that all these things I was

---

4   Saligari, M. (2017, May). Feelings: Handle Them Before They Handle You. TedTalks. Retrieved from https://www.youtube.com/watch?v=JD4O7ama3o8.

doing for other people, you know - when I thought I was being a good person and doing the right thing, when I was people-pleasing and trying to save everyone and trying to be there for everyone and trying to make everyone happy and trying to help everyone solve their problems - I thought I was doing it all out of the goodness of my heart. That was my conscious understanding anyway.

But I realized that I wasn't doing it out of the goodness of my heart. There was a childhood wound in me that led me to seek validation from others. I was seeking that pat on the back. Those words, "You're such a good person. Thank you. You've helped me and I'm so grateful." I was looking for reassurance. I was looking for my self-worth cup to be filled by someone or something outside of me.

So this emotional trigger turned into one of the most freeing experiences of my life - because I was no longer imprisoned by this unconscious need to please (and be validated) by others.

And this kind of soul freedom is what I want for you.

First and foremost, I want you to focus on joy - on living joy and experiencing joy and appreciating joy and creating joy and basking in joy. But when moment comes up when you are triggered, I want you to be grateful for that, too, because you are about to experience a healing and a release, if you're open to it.

Our emotions are our inner guidance system. When we're feeling good, when we're feeling happy, when we're feeling joyful, we're on the path of least resistance. When we're feeling triggered, a sliver is coming up to be acknowledged, healed, and released.

If you find yourself on a path of resistance (anger, sadness, self-doubt, etc.) start to ask yourself what would excite you now. What would make you happy? What would you look forward to? What would you love to create? What would you love to work toward? Find the support you need to help you get where you want to be. Often we need someone outside of us to pull us beyond the version of ourselves we're currently stuck in.

Be grateful for this powerful inner guidance system that you have, but allow yourself to be human and release any emotions that are no longer serving you. Acknowledge them, allow them to flow through you, and release them.

Instead of depleting yourself in the name of helping others - fill your happy, joyful, fulfilling, soul-nourishing cups up all the way over the brim, and then serve others from your overflow. In this way, you are your best, brightest, and happiest you - which also happens to be the most powerful and inspiring way you could ever serve others, too.

*Doing what you love
is the cornerstone of
having abundance in your life.
~ Dr. Wayne Dyer*

CHAPTER 18

Awakening Your Wealth: How To Be Richer and Happier Starting Today

"You are a living magnet. What you attract into your life is in harmony with your dominant thoughts."
~ Brian Tracy

Just last week I was meditating on one of my favorite beaches in La Jolla, California, and a message came through: *Money follows joy, joy does not follow money.*

As with all the insights that download during my meditations, this struck me as absolute truth. When I connect the dots of my past - from having my nine-to-five in finance to starting my photography business to spending a year full-time in network marketing and then moving on to my online coaching and spiritual teaching business - the times that I have been the wealthiest and most financially successful have been the times that joy and purpose were my priority. Money was almost just an afterthought; purpose and passion were in the driver's seat, and profits were in the passenger side.

The times when money was at the forefront of my mind were the times when I felt the most broke, struggling, and hard-working. These are also the times when I was doing things completely out of alignment in order to try and bring more money into my life. So many of us tie our sense of happiness, our sense of freedom, our sense of joy, and maybe even our sense of self-worth to money. We believe that when we have just a little bit more money, we will be so much happier. Life will be so much easier. We will finally be able to exhale and enjoy our life.

So we focus on attaining more money, we are willing to work jobs we don't love. We are willing to create things in our business that don't actually light us up, but that we think will sell. We're willing to alter who we are and what we say. We think by doing this, we'll attract more money and we can finally be happy.

But what ends up happening is that we become an inauthentic, out-of-alignment version of ourselves - one who is unhappy, unfulfilled, and likely not feeling very rich at all.

It can feel very counterintuitive to put the focus of money in the passenger seat when we're so attached to thinking and believing that more money is the path to freedom. What I really want for you to understand as you read these words and even after you finish this book is that when you are willing to lose sight of the shore and let go of the anchor (that is, the need to focus on creating more money), when you explore what's beyond that need and that fear and you sail toward purpose and joy and excitement, you will inevitably become richer in all ways, including financially, than you've ever been before.

Fortune favors the aligned.

When you are doing something that excites you and that you love, you radiate passion, excitement, enthusiasm, joy - and that energy is absolutely magnetic. People will turn their heads and wonder what it is that you're doing. How you can be so happy. And how they can create this happiness for themselves as well. They'll want to learn from you. They'll want to watch you. They'll want to work with you. They'll want to buy whatever it is you're using.

The Universe, too, will feel your higher vibration and will send to you more things of higher vibration. Yes, including more money. This sense of happiness, purpose, fulfillment, momentum, and alignment will not only increase your abundance financially, it will also affect all areas of your life. You will become rich not only in money but in love, fulfillment, joy, ecstasy, and purpose. Isn't that what you really wanted all along anyway?

I once explained this concept to my clients as being similar to the way that you would kick a soccer ball.

When my stepdad was first teaching me how to kick a soccer ball, I was eight years old and I kept looking down at my foot and the ball. I figured that's what you're supposed to do. If you want your foot to hit the ball, then you've got to look down at your foot and the ball. And he said, "No, no, Jen, look up toward where you want the ball to go, and your foot will know what to do." This felt really counterintuitive to me. I thought, "No, I need to focus on my foot! I need to look at where my foot is hitting the ball so I can aim for where it's going."

Again, he said, "No, no, Jen, just trust me. I've done this before, I know a thing or two . . . Look where you want the ball to go and your foot will know what to do . . ."

So I stubbornly tried it my way a few times and the ball kept going haywire. Once in a while, it might go where I had hoped it would, but most of the time it was going off to the side or too far or not far enough. But when I took his advice and I looked where I wanted to kick the ball, what my main objective was for the ball, there it went, every single time.

It's like this with money, too. Sometimes we think we need to look directly at the money. In order to create more of it, we need to figure out the exact right place to create it, to earn it. So we stare right at it. That's like staring at the foot and the ball. What I'm inviting you to at least try is to instead focus on the outcome that you believe more money will create for you and your life. It's not the actual piece of paper that you want. It's not the digital number on a computer screen that you want. It's the feeling you think you're going to have once you see that dollar amount in your bank account. So what is that for you? What is it that you believe you're going to feel when you have more money? Are you going to feel freedom? Are you going to feel peace? Are you going to feel generous? Adventurous? Excited? Grateful?

What are the top two or three things that you believe you will feel when you have more money? List them below now.

1. _____
2. _____
3. _____

What I encourage you to do is start focusing on those feelings, on that outcome, on that destination. Instead of staring down at your feet, the ball, the money - look ahead at what you believe you'll feel once you have it and at where you want your life to go. Next, I want you to start noticing where you feel that way in your life already, even if it's in smaller ways and for a fleeting moment here and there.

If you believe freedom is one of the things that you'll feel when you have more money, where in your life do you feel freedom already? Now you might be thinking, "Jen, I don't have any freedom. That's why I want more money!" But I encourage you to go a little deeper. Recall Chapter 12, the numerous ways and moments you have freedom in your life: freedom of choice, freedom to live, breathe, socialize, and more. Focus on those moments, truly being grateful for those types of freedom, and watch how more of the good stuff appears!

Or maybe it's joy. Maybe you believe when you have more money, you will be happier. And so instead of thinking to yourself, *I'll be happy when I have more money* (which is the same as thinking, *I'm not happy right now*, and guess what? The Universe is listening to you and your vibration of, *I'm not happy right now* and giving you more things to not be happy about), focus on where you *do* feel happiness and joy already. Even if you're in debt, even if you're living paycheck to paycheck, even if you're barely scraping by, even if you're really concerned about your finances, where are the moments in your life where you are experiencing joy? Joy can take on many forms - it can be a hug from a loved one, just being out in nature, it can be moving your body in a way that empowers you, or it can be the simple pleasure of a cup of coffee and a good book or movie. For every form of joy you encounter, give thanks to the Universe and embrace those moments. You will find that there is more joy present in your life than you even realize. Trust me, there are ways for you to feel joy and happiness right now.

No matter what your financial situation is, the more you focus on being happy now, the easier it is for the Universe to bring you more of that which will make you happy, including money.

One of the things that really helped me shift my perception of money and start welcoming more abundance into my life is when I started seeing money as someone I was in a relationship with. I thought about how I was acting and behaving in this relationship. Was I acting needy? Was I acting desperate? I would never want to act like that in a real-life relationship. *Because how attractive is that?!* So why would I be acting like that with my relationship with money?

I was in this space of "I don't need money. I'm fine without money. I don't need money in order to be happy." And then in the next breath, I would be thinking, "But oh man, I wish I had more money. Why don't I have money? Why doesn't money hang out with me? Where are you, money? I need you. Why aren't you here? But I don't need you because I'm not shallow and I'm not materialistic. But I sure could use some more money right now . . ." Can you see what a confusing message that is to be putting out into the Universe? Money is energy. Money is currency. Money is paying attention to your vibration. Are you magnetizing it or are you repelling it?

The way to magnetize money - or anything else - is to be attractive to it. Be the kind of person with whom someone (money) would be excited to be in a relationship with. Do you respect money? Save some, give some, and play with some? Do you have fun together? Do you do meaningful things together? Do you let it go when it feels called to be invested somewhere? Do you trust it will always be there to support you when you need it?

If you were money, would YOU want to be in a relationship with you?

When you become more open to receiving more money, make sure to notice and celebrate every single penny, every single dime, every single dollar. Celebrate money in all its many forms. If you're new to being open to receiving, which many women are, just be open to receiving compliments at first. If someone compliments you, instead of deflecting or placing the credit somewhere else, accept the compliment with a simple thank you. Don't shoot a compliment back to the person or deflect it in any way. Allow it to land. Receive it. Just say thank you.

When you see a penny on the ground, pick it up. Thank the Universe and know that more is on the way. When you go to a checkout counter for your groceries or clothes or some other purchase and something was on sale that you didn't even realize was on sale, thank the Universe. When someone wants to pay for your coffee, your lunch or your dinner, or give you a gift, *let them - without running out to buy them a gift in return.* Give a silent thank you to the Big U, because that was another way it was sending you abundance. The Universe is sending more and more forms of money your way as you begin to notice and appreciate it more.

You may receive a surprise check in the mail. Maybe your tax return was bigger than you were expecting or arrives sooner than you thought. Maybe someone to whom you lent money that you completely forgot about is finally paying you back. Maybe you get an idea for your business, and suddenly you are creating something brand new that you weren't expecting and generating unplanned income. There's so many infinite ways for the Universe to bring blessings and abundance to you. You've just got to be open to receiving it, open to seeing it, and open to appreciating it.

Being in a state of gratitude, appreciation, and openness to receive is magnetic. Here's an exercise you can put into practice to help you receive money from the Universe. *(I also have a free workbook called the Monthly Money Manifestor, available at jenniferjayde.com/theawakeningbook)*

Step #1:

Make a list of your non-negotiable expenses for the month. This means your bills, your minimum payments, your rent / mortgage, your car payment, a dollar amount for groceries, all your non-negotiable needs. Add it all up.

Step #2:

Ask your inner guide, "What would be the most exciting way(s) that I could create or receive this income this month?" Make a note that you're open to this amount, or higher. You're open to the Universe surprising you and making it even easier and more joyful.

Step #3:

Make a T-chart. On one side, put "my inspired action," and on the other side, put "the Universe." Under "my inspired action", write down ideas that come up for you to create space, to welcome this income into your reality so that you can look to the Universe for guidance. If you're an entrepreneur, maybe you wrote down gaining some new clients this month with one-on-one offerings or a course or a program. If you're in a job, part time or full-time - this income may come from your paycheck. Maybe you have a side hustle you'd love to use to create some extra income. Maybe there's a bonus at your company that you could work toward. But don't limit yourself either. Know that money can come from anywhere, and it doesn't have to come from where you think it should.

So what are you feeling called to do to come to the table and meet the Universe halfway in creating this income and welcoming it into your life? You might continue to receive some more ideas or inspirations along the way even after you've created this list.

On "the Universe" side, you've got a couple options. You can either leave it blank to signify that you trust. You know the Universe is going to do everything in its limitless power to support you in this. Or you can jot down some things to remind you that the Universe is capable of anything you could write down. Maybe the Universe is going to connect you with the right people.

Maybe that it's going to help your potential clients see your posts. Maybe it's going to surprise and delight you in more ways than you can even imagine.

Now you can place an "on or before" date when you'd like to manifest and welcome this money into your life. If you do this, I very much encourage you to remain detached from the outcome once this date rolls around. Absolutely ask for what you want, but trust in whatever is given and then go from there.

I start this process by plugging my number into my New Reality morning recording each month. For example, I say, "Thank you for my _____ ($1,000, as an example) _____ in income from September 1st to September 30th, 20__."

Then think about what I could do to create that thousand dollars of income in the most joyful way. In my online coaching business, this could be one-on-one coaching or an online program or a course. Then I jot down what I need to do to open up my funnel to receiving. Do I feel inspired to create some Facebook ads, create an affiliate offering, make some posts on social media, reach out to warm potential clients, etc. I list whatever I'm feeling called to do from an inspired place, not a desperate one. I also think about whether I need to hire a mentor or business coach to support me with this goal.

Then each month, I up the ante a little bit. The first month I ever did this, I was just looking for $1,000 in coaching income. The second month, I bumped it to $3,000, then the next to $5,000, then $10,000 and so on. I was very consistent with this, and I was consistent with listening to my morning recording and with putting in the inspired action and following my own inner GPS.

I also really encourage you to remain open to receiving money from all different sources and to noticing when it's coming in all different forms. Give appreciation for that and remain detached from the outcome. If you create an income intention for the month and you don't hit it, trust that it is for good reason. Trust that everything is always working out for you, and feel into where you want to go from there. Was the number bigger than your belief? Were you committed? Were you consistent? Were you ready to receive that amount? Truly ready? What vibration were you holding? What thoughts were you thinking? What action were you taking? Consistency is key. Being open to receiving is key. Being grateful for every single dollar, every single surprise, every single sale is key.

But being truly joyful and grateful in this moment is your absolute path of least resistance to more joy, more abundance, and more freedom.

Fortune favors the aligned.
~ Jennifer Jayde

CHAPTER 19

Rise And Shine (Awakened)

"Someone who takes the time to understand their relationship with source, who actively seeks alignment with their broader perspective, who deliberately seeks and finds alignment with who they really are, is more charismatic, more attractive, more effective, and more powerful than a group of millions who have not achieved this alignment."
~ Esther Hicks

If I never write another book, there are some things that I would love to leave you with. I used to be the person who wanted to know all the answers right now, right away, the woman who wanted to overachieve as fast as possible so she could finally relax and enjoy her life. I was a type A perfectionist, a control freak, and I could never meet my own expectations. I was impatient with myself. I was always caught up thinking about the future, and I was always rushing from one moment to the next. It took a devastating loss in my family to put an end to that version of myself and to finally awaken to the fact that every single moment is precious and every single moment should be savored. I am grateful every single day that my eyes are open now. My soul is open now, and even though my life is not at the pinnacle of all my hopes and dreams in this present moment, I love my life just the way it is, right now. It's so freeing to know that you can love your life in this present moment - even if it's not perfect, even before you've reached the next destination, even if you're in debt, even if you feel overweight, even if you're single and wishing you weren't, even you desire more money, a bigger house, more freedom. You can still be so in love with your life in this very moment. When you're in that energy of loving your life and seeing all of the blessings you really do already have, you are pouring gasoline on the fire of your dreams.

It's not the forcing. It's not the grinding. It's not the hustling. It is the joy in the present moment that speeds you into momentum for even greater joy.

I was at a motivational conference in Las Vegas a couple of years ago, and the speaker told us to take a pen and draw a tiny pinpoint dot on a blank piece of paper. He said, "Put that dot right up to your eyeball now. This dot represents the things that aren't going your way, the things that you look unfavorably upon in your life."

He continued along the lines of, "Most people live staring at this one tiny dot and allow it to consume them and to consume their whole life and to consume their energy. This then creates a domino effect into the other areas of their life. Just zoom out, pull the paper away from your face and look at all that white space. Look at all the amazing things you do have going for you that you've likely been overlooking and taking for granted." We would be a far happier human race if we would choose to focus on our blessings rather than our burdens.

To my soul sibling reading this book, thank you for going along on this journey with me. I want you to know that you are an infinite limitless being, that you are so much more powerful, capable, strong, and freer than you realize. You are not just a human who can only rely on human strengths and human abilities and human thoughts and human beliefs. You are a divine, spiritual being capable of anything. The only thing getting in your way is you.

Any time you hear a voice telling you that you can't do something, that you'll never be able to achieve this or do that, you're not her, you're not him, this will never happen, you're going to stay in debt forever, your dreams will never come true - recognize that those are lies. The truth is that what you want, what is in your heart is meant for you. The desire, the vision, the purpose wouldn't have been given to you if it wasn't meant to be yours. So yes, you are capable. Yes, it is possible and yes, you can do it. Reach out and get the support you need. If you find you're not able to do it on your own, we are stronger together. We are powerful when we link arms, and together we can achieve anything.

You are a divine, spiritual being
capable of anything.
The only thing getting in your way is you.
~ Jennifer Jayde

Remember, no more effort
is required to aim high in life,
to demand abundance and
prosperity than is required
to accept misery and poverty.
- Napoleon Hill

*Fight for your dreams,
not your limitations.
~ Jennifer Jayde*

FINAL MESSAGE

Hello kindred soul,

I have a very important message for you today. It has to do with you, your mission here, and the time you have left. You see, beautiful spirit, your birth was no accident. Even if you were told you were an accident - trust me - the Universe never makes mistakes.

The truth is, even though we are timeless souls, our physical time here to complete our lessons, our soul growth, and our unique and powerful contribution to the world is indeed finite.

My friend, there is no more time to waste in fear, second-guessing, over analyzing, procrastinating, and above all else, self-doubt. Your time has come.

Your time is now.

So what can we do when we're spinning our wheels in the quicksand of self-doubt?

Learn to trust. I mean really, really trust. I know what you might be thinking things like, "That's great, Jen, but I have mouths to feed, people depending on me, and no special talents to speak of. I know my spouse secretly thinks my ideas are silly, I'll disappoint my parents if I don't do what they see as safe and secure."

This is our good ol' ego (inner critic) popping up, turning up the volume because we're moving further and further away from its control over us.

A friend of mine works in palliative care as a nurse (for people who are about to pass over into their next adventure). She said that just before we die, often times we get a surge of energy. It's like our body's way of giving everything it has left to fight death just one last time. This often confuses loved ones into thinking the patient is getting better, only to have them die very shortly after.

And I've realized, ego is very similar to this. When it feels we are no longer fueling it and giving it our attention (empowering it), it starts to lose its power over us. It starts to die. So it will surge up with whatever energy it has left to try and win you back. Win you back to self-doubt, overthinking, overanalyzing, fearing, etc. so that you will stay right where you are or, even better, retreat to where you were. Into the familiar, the recognizable, the safe zone.

So acknowledge that this is happening.

You can even thank ego for doing its job and trying to protect you. Maybe even picture it like an annoying older sibling or a nagging mother or mother-in-law. They think they're doing what's best for you out of love . . . even if it doesn't always feel that way.

So be grateful, but also let ego know that it's okay. "We're okay, and regardless of what you say, I'm moving forward . . . so you might as well give it a rest." Then shift your attention away from how you don't want to feel and focus on how you DO want to feel. Refocus your attention away from "I, me, myself, what if this happens to me, my family . . . " and focus on your *why* and how it will serve so many people, including your loved ones. You will do the best you can right from the start, and you will only get better from there.

Your confidence will come from action, getting your hands wet with experience, and *feeling the fear and doing it anyway.*

It won't come from thinking about things and trying to think yourself into feeling more confident. Trust me. If we wait until we feel ready, *we'll be waiting for the rest of our lives.*

So put one foot in front of the other, keep moving forward. Attach to your WHY. Who else will benefit from a happier, more fulfilled, more excited, more ignited, more alive version of you?! And who else? And who else? And how will that effect ripple out from there?!

Then think about the alternative. Would you rather move forward despite any fear or unknowns and see what's possible in the time you have left? Or would you prefer to fold now and never know what could've been?

Make your decision. There's no right or wrong answer.

Then OWN IT. I'm here for you!

You've got this! No looking back. <3

Follow your heart always,

Jen xoxo

*Don't die with your music
still in you.
~ Dr. Wayne Dyer*

Far better to see what's possible, than to always wonder what could've been . . .
~ Jennifer Jayde

ACKNOWLEDMENTS

My first solo book would not have been possible without the amazing dedication, talent, skill, and brilliance of Ky-Lee Hanson and her team at Golden Brick Road Publishing House. You are truly masters at what you do, and lead with your hearts in everything you create. Thank you for your guidance, patience, and love throughout this entire process. There are not enough words to express my gratitude for you. Thank you for empowering myself and countless fellow authors now to share their message, love and light with the world. You truly are angels in disguise. Thank you. I love you.

ABOUT THE AUTHOR

Jennifer Jayde is an international speaker, author, and mentor who connects women from around the globe with their purpose and supports them in creating soul aligned businesses, knowing from experience that when your work ignites your soul - you will light up the world.

She comes from humble beginnings - a small town girl from Canada whose earliest memory was sharing a bedroom with her single mom in an old basement suite. At age twenty-two, she became a 100% commission-based mortgage broker, and grew her business to generate over six figures in total annual sales.

By age twenty-six, she had a serious wake up call and realized her soul was pulling her to follow her childhood passion of photography. She left the mortgage industry and began her full time business, specializing in destination weddings. Jennifer became a top photographer in her region, garnering consecutive awards for her work.

She then felt the familiar "tap on the shoulder," and followed her passion once again. This time, in helping women around the world find their purpose and truly live limitlessly.

Within a few short months of starting her coaching business, she sold out her 1:1 coaching program, waitlisted her group program, and generated over a quarter million in sales in her first year of business, helping women around the world discover their purpose and truly create their dream lives.

She now resides in sunny San Diego, but feels at home wherever there is sunshine and salty air.

www.jenniferjayde.com
ig: jenniferjayde_successcoach
fb: jenniferjaydedreambizcoach

GOLDEN BRICK ROAD
PUBLISHING HOUSE

Locking arms and helping each other down
their Golden Brick Road

At Golden Brick Road Publishing House, we lock arms with ambitious people and create success through a collaborative, supportive, and accountable environment. We are a boutique shop that caters to all stages of business around a book. We encourage women empowerment, and gender and cultural equality by publishing single author works from around the world, and creating in-house collaborative author projects for emerging and seasoned authors to join.

Our authors have a safe space to grow and diversify themselves within the genres of poetry, health, sociology, women's studies, business, and personal development. We help those who are natural born leaders, step out and shine! Even if they do not yet fully see it for themselves. We believe in empowering each individual who will then go and inspire an entire community. Our Director, Ky-Lee Hanson, calls this: The Inspiration Trickle Effect.

If you want to be a public figure that is focused on helping people and providing value, but you do not want to embark on the journey alone, then we are the community for you.

To inquire about our collaborative writing opportunities or to bring your own idea into fruition, reach out to us at:

www.goldenbrickroad.pub

Connect with our authors and readers at GBRSociety.com